SHAMANS

WHO WORK WITH THE LIGHT

The Power of Shamanic Lightworking to Help You Find Your Truth and Heal the World

MAYA COINTREAU

An Earth Lodge® Publication
http://www.earthlodgebooks.com
Roxbury, Connecticut

This book contains valuable and carefully researched information, but it is not intended to take the place of proper medical care. Please seek qualified professional care for mental and physical health problems.

Copyright 2017 by Maya Cointreau
Printed & Published in the United States by Earth Lodge

ISBN 978-1-944396-38-1

All rights reserved, including the right to reproduce this work in any form whatsoever, without written permission, except in the case of brief quotation in critical articles or reviews. All information in this Earth Lodge book is based upon the experiences of the author. For information contact Earth Lodge®, 12 Church Street, Roxbury, CT 06783 or visit Earth Lodge® online at www.earthlodgebooks.com.

Cover Artwork, Layout & Design by Maya Cointreau

*To my students,
the most amazing shamanic lightworkers
who have graced my path.*

You taught me.

Table of Contents

What is a Shaman? 1

Connecting to the Earth 14

Chakras & Breathwork.. 30

The Energy of Air... 48

Fire that Moves Us 58

Flowing with the Water Element 73

Navigating Dream Worlds 88

Ether: The Fifth Element 105

Clearing Distortion in the Akashic Realm 108

The Sacred Hoop... 122

Sticks & Stones 135

Harmonizing with Sound 171

Healing the Soul 184

Healing is an Art 205

Honoring the Ancestors... 220

The Shamanic Lightworker's Toolkit 225

Is Light and Dark the Same as Good and Evil? 233

Freeing the True You 251

Be the Light 260

What is a Shaman?

A Shaman is a person who works with the realm of Spirit, with Energy, to benefit his or her community. The community might be their family, their circle of friends, their village, country or the planet. Shamans intercede with the ancestors, gods and spirits, with nature and the earth, on behalf of their community. This has been the primary charge of shamans in every culture since time immemorial. It is a shaman's task to help others, to create a better environment for their community (as large or small as it may be), to heal rifts and improve life conditions.

Shamans are aware of the energetic flow and patterns of the universe, they acknowledge the spirit through that works through everything, and they in turn work with that spirit and flow to shift the world. The word "shaman" is Siberian in origin, but there have been shamans in every culture on Earth throughout the ages, medicine people who can connect with Source, or Spirit, to heal and create balance in the world.

Through these pages you will gather the tools needed to walk a balanced path towards self-empowerment, exploring core shamanism and healing techniques from around the globe. At the end you will have a clearer, stronger understanding of you: an empowered and integrated person whose soul and physical life is in harmony, whose very existence helps clear mass consciousness and improve the quality of all life on earth. You will have joined the ranks of the lightworkers, who work with the light for the highest good of all beings. Lightworkers understand the interconnectedness of all things, all beings, and strive to create a more harmonious, light-based realm on Earth. "Light" shamanism focuses on techniques that can be used heal oneself and the community on multiple levels.

Over the last several centuries human populations have grown while shamans have decreased, creating an imbalance in the world. It is our job, as spirit workers, to restore that balance. Among other things, shamanic work can be used to help cleanse pollution; stabilize weather patterns; heal mental, spiritual and physical disease; harmonize living spaces; and create better work relationships. It is our responsibility to intercede with spirit for the good of the community.

As shamans, we are dealing with real and potent sources of power.

Never underestimate the power of a single shamanic meditation. Everything you do helps to raise the vibration of your community, of mass consciousness and the earth. Each small act of balance shifts the web of humanity and helps to create a better world. As a shamanic person of power and Great Spirit, your responsibility to the earth grows, too. Spirit recognizes spirit. A "lay-person" can get away with acts of pollution or disrespect and still visit a lake to catch some fish with success. A shaman will be recognized by the spirits of the lake, and if they do not first display respect or give thanks and blessings in some small way, it is unlikely they will catch even a single sunfish.

As you embark on this journey of learning, know that the spirits are watching you. They are joyful to know that more humans are reawakening to the magic of their souls. But they are also waiting, and watching, to see how you will be helping to restore balance and rejoin in the act of co-creation that man has always had with Spirit.

Meditation and the Drum

Shamans around the world have long used drums, rattles, song and dance to quickly reach deep trance states. Scientific studies have shown that repetitive heartbeat style drumming quickly shifts brain waves to a deep meditative dream state that resonates with the same frequency as the earth itself. When we drum, we dream, and we are in full vibrational alignment with the earth's living matrix. When this happens, we come into alignment with our birth purpose, with our soul's intentions and the most positive wishes of mass consciousness.

If you have a hard time meditating, chances are shamanic journeying will be easier for you. When you journey, you aren't turning off your thoughts – you are freeing them, enhancing them. Drums and rattles quell our ego and relax our body, allowing our inner self to soar freely into the realms of spirit. It is here that we can gain insight, wisdom, healing and guidance, right from Spirit.

If you have a drum or a rattle, practice drumming yourself into meditation. No fancy skills are needed, just maintain a steady, regular rhythm that reminds you of the beats of your feet hitting the ground while you walk – it is this rhythm that will help keep you on track during your travels. A good length of time to spend on your journey is somewhere between 10-30 minutes – if you are drumming yourself, simply return when you feel complete. If you are drumming for someone other than yourself, you will need to add what is called a "call back" to the end of the journey. A call back lets people know that it is time to thank their guides and return swiftly back into their bodies. This is achieved by hitting the drum slowly four times, and then hitting the drum double time for 30-60 seconds, as if the foot-beats are now running, and then a final four, slow beats to signal the journey's end.

If you find drumming or rattling for yourself difficult, you can use this free audio track that I have created for you here: http://enchantedrealmz.com/learning/JourneyingTrackwithRemoGoddessDrum.mp3

Meeting Your Guides

One of the first things we want to do as new shamans is to meet some of our power animals or guides. The more work you do in the shamanic realms (or indeed, with any sort of spiritual, meditative or healing work), the more guides you are likely to meet. Each guide is different, and can help you with different things. Some guides will help you travel quickly through dark realms or to find the dead or the lost. Some guides will teach you to fly or swim. Some are adept at healing, and will teach you their particular branch of healing. Some will help you find your voice, some know how to dance through time and space.

When Native Americans say the words "all my ancestors" as a prayer, they don't just refer to their family, but also to the previous worlds and races of men that came before them, to the animals, the plants, and the stones. Animals, by virtually all spiritual and archaeological accounts, were here before us. Just as the "stone people", the rocks and crystals, carry ancient knowledge, the animals carry great wisdom. They know how the world works. They know how to navigate through all domains of Mother Earth. They also have remained more interconnected than we have, and can talk more easily with each other, and thus have access to a greater web of knowledge than we do.

An animal guide might be the high-level soul of an actual animal we have known (cat with a small c), or it might more of a collective representation of that species (Deer with a capital D). One is not better than the other, just different. The former is friend, a partner. The latter is more of an ally who is willing to lend you some of its knowledge and power in return for something (company, prayer, offerings, songs, dance, are all good starts). Sometimes, a guide will ask you to do something for them, like pick up trash or visit a particular place. Genetically, we all have Animals who have allied with our clans through the ages -- even if not in recent centuries -- so often those Animals return to us when we begin to study shamanism.

As far as other kinds of guides go, there are many out there. Some people connect with other planetary races. Some people speak with ascended spiritual masters (saints, Buddha, Mary Magdalene, etc.). Some work with gods and goddesses from other religions, some work with familial ancestors, some work with aspects of their own souls from past lives, some work with angels and elemental spirits like the winds or thunder people. There are many, many possibilities, and you're just starting to meet your guides. The most important thing is to remain open to whomever (or whatever) you might meet. Remember that teachers come in all forms and sizes.

Meditation to Create Your Place of Power

As you learn to journey it's easiest to have a private, special place of power that you can always start from, a place where you know you're power animals and guides will always be ready to meet you, a place that fills your heart with joy and excites you. To begin, let's embark on a journey to discover what this perfect place is, for you. It might be a real location that you've been to many times or read about just once. It might be a place you've never imagined, or it might be your back yard. It might be a temple in Asia, some standing stones in Europe, a pasture in Connecticut or a dock by a lake. It might be a desert cave or a jungle forest. The more you journey, the more places you will collect. I have many places I journey from, depending on where I'm planning to go, just as I have many guides that work with me, depending on what our mission is that day. But we all have a special place that will always be our first gathering point, our first power spot, that holds a special place in our heart. So let's put on some quiet music and begin our meditation now to find yours.

I want you to breathe in, nice and deeply, and then let it go. Breathe in the fresh, joyful energy of the day, and let out all your fears or worries. Breathe in the beauty. Breathe out the stress.

Breathe in, and breathe out.

In, and out. In, and out.

With each breathe in, I want you to go deeper within your body. Breathe in, and go inside, deep into the darkness. Breathe in, and go down, down into yourself. Breathe in, and go deeper, until you reach your inner point of stillness.

Deep within your self is a still point, a quiet darkness where creation begins. Here, anything is possible. You are a god within your own body.

In the darkness, you rise up, and begin to walk east, into the gentle dawn of morning. The light ahead of you glows gently, drawing you forward. Slowly, a landscape begins to form, and as you walk you begin to see details before you. As you walk, the light grows brighter, the sun rising over the horizon, and you find yourself approaching your place of power, your gathering point, the place where all your journeys will begin from.

Relax, and explore this place. You might want to sit quietly in the space and meditate, getting comfortable with its energy. You might want to create a small altar in the place or explore the area. Call out for your guides, asking to meet a high vibrational spirit of the light – it could be a power animal, an ancestor, a god, an angel or even your higher self. If you happen to see any people or animals, ask them if they are your guides or if they have any messages for you. Use this time to become comfortable in your space and the journey realm.

Connecting to the Earth

The Earth Element is associated most prominently with dark, earthy colors: black, red, brown. Green evokes the life-giving energy of the earth element. When someone is out of balance with the earth element they will often be described as flighty, spacey or hyperactive. They might suffer from joint and muscle pain, be stubborn, overly cautious or fearful. Feel like you have rocks in your shoulders? Maybe your muscles are trying to remind you to connect to the earth element.

As we've discussed, a shaman is a person who works with the realm of Spirit, with Energy, to benefit the world and her community. So what happens if a shaman is not connected to the earth element? Often, their work may begin to feel meaningless and undirected, not to mention their own energy. Grounding is not really about getting energy from the earth - the Earth is not the best or ultimate Source of energy for a human being, especially now. The best source of energy for a human being is Source. Earth Energy does have a special benefit though, in that it connects us more fully to physical reality – this is what being grounded really means.

When you are grounded, the energy of Source can flow through you at optimum levels improving your physical incarnation – your body and your reality – here on Earth.

The planet, as we know, is going through her own growing pains. She is shifting and raising her own vibrations, and sometimes she, too feels grumpy and uncomfortable. Grounding is good, but over the last couple decades connecting deeply to the Earth has become less predictable – it is now even more possible to pick up her unrest and dissatisfaction, especially if you are very empathic. Be mindful of how you feel after Earth-work, and know when to disconnect.

Shamans have always performed Earth-work to benefit the planet, whether on a regional or a world-wide scale. These days Earth-work is more important than ever. Perform the following tree ritual to feed the planet while you rejuvenate yourself. If you sense the planet is especially unbalanced while you are working, take in additional Source energy through the top of your head, fueled by the light of Source and the heat of the Sun to feed and harmonize the planet.

Imagine You Are a Tree

Sit straight and tall, and breathe deeply. Imagine you are taking in air through all your pores, not just your lungs.

Feel the oxygen entering your bloodstream and clearing out debris while it energizes your entire body, cell by cell. When you breathe out, toxins and stale air leave your body.

Breathe in and out.

Now imagine you have roots flowing out through your feet, your root chakra, your spine. Visualize a long tap root reaching far down, down into the earth. Feel the earth alive and pulsing with energy all around your root, the energy flowing freely up the root and into you through the soles of your feet and your root chakra. The earth energy flows up through your chakras, through your body, and connects you to the Earth. You feel loved and connected. As the earth energy flows through your body, through your torso, your head, your arms and legs, it relaxes you and releases feelings of stress and anxiety you've been storing on a cellular, muscular level. Any stressed or tired energy you have flows is released down through your root chakra, through your tap root, and eliminated into the earth. You sense the cells of the earth, the organisms living in the soil, are eager to be nourished by this energy, and that they will use it to create new, clean energy for you. Allow this circle of energy to flow for several minutes, taking in the clear energy of the earth, and releasing your old, tired, used energy to feed her and be renewed.

When you feel completely clear and recharged, thank the earth, gather up your taproot, and return. This is a good time to offer additional food to the earth – cornmeal, tobacco or beer are traditional gifts in many traditions.

Walking Cleanse

You can use this method anytime you are walking or exercising, whether you are indoors or outdoors. As you walk, breathe deeply. Imagine that the air you breathe is pure, perfect, clean. As it enters your aura, any pollutants are purified by the white light that surrounds you. Breathe in the air. Every breath fills your body with energy, oxygenates your lungs and emboldens your soul. You are pure light, and every breath you take makes you lighter and lighter. Every time your foot hits the ground, imagine excess energy pulsing off of you, releasing in small atomic bursts. As you raise your foot up, you draw the energy of the earth to you, into you. You are grounded. Clear. Free.

Foods that can help with grounding

Although all foods are, on some level, grounding, certain foods are better than others at stimulating the root chakra, while other foods work better on higher chakras. Also, keep in mind that each body is different. Your body may react differently to certain foods than the rest of your friends or family. Pay attention to what works for you.

Root vegetables and high-protein foods are the most grounding. Potatoes, beets, carrots, turnips, celeriac, eggs, meat, nuts and beans are just a few examples of such foods. These foods help seat us firmly in our lower chakras and fuel us with large amounts of grounding earth energy. Dried foods are also very grounding, whether they are meat, vegetable or fruit, due to their archetypal connection to survival in the mass consciousness.

To clear your root and sacral chakras, eat spices like horseradish and hot peppers, garlic and onions. On the sweet side, sugar and honey are also grounding and calming, while chocolate literally repels negative energy. Salty foods, and salt itself, encourage our ability to receive energy from the earth and the sun, and let our body's energy centers flow as intended. Dairy will slow the flow of energy within the body, helping those who have an over-abundance of energy running through them to better utilize the information they are receiving. Dairy can also reduce energy leakage and enhance psychic reception.

Clothes and Your Environment

Certain colors and materials can also help you ground. Try wearing earth tones and natural fabrics derived from plants or animals to help you connect to the earth. Your furniture, the color of your walls, all these can have a profound effect on both your biofield and your mindset. A room decorated in forest-like colors can be as nurturing as a the real thing, helping you rest and recharge, especially in the dead of winter or the high heat of summer.

Pyramid or Circle of Light

One of the most basic yet effective methods of protection is to imagine yourself surrounded by white light. Many traditions like the effect of a circle or dome of light. To both protect yourself and raise your energy, a pyramid is effective.

Visualize a white pyramid of light in front of you, and then see yourself walking into it. See the light seal behind you. Set the intention that can enter in without your consent that is harmful to you. You can also use this visualization to protect your house or the room you are in. To protect very large spaces, I find domes to be very effective. Sometimes you might see the light as another color, such as blue or purple. That is OK too. The key to creating an effective thought-form is your intent.

In all ritual work, especially in visualizations, you must begin with clear intentions. Whatever you intend, you will achieve. If you want to do something, but do not believe in it with every fiber of your being, you will not have an easy time achieving it. The key is *intent*. *Intent* is more than just sort of, kind of, wanting to do something. Intent is about really wanting it. Really *meaning* it. Intent is about clarity of purpose, single-mindedness of will. As Yoda so aptly put it in *Star Wars*: "Do, or do not. There is no try." Never set out to "try" something. It most likely will not get finished, and it will not be pleasant, either: related to the punitive words trial, or test, as it is. Set out to *do* everything, and things will get done. An easy way to work with developing your intentions is to simply state them. Say out loud "I intend to..."

Mountain Protection

For really solid, earthy protection, try grounding through mountain terrain. Do the same tree meditation, but imagine yourself on top of a mountain you feel connected to. Imagine your roots going down through and around the deep, substantial rocks that make the heart of the mountain. This can be a longer, more difficult process as your roots meet with more resistance, but they also connect you to the tough, immovable, extremely stable energy of the mountain. If you feel like the mountain you are trying to connect with is grumpy, demanding or inhospitable, try another mountain.

Remember that we have a moral obligation as shamans to use our power for good. Remember that our guides are not us, or controlled by us. Guides in some cultures are called allies, and as such they agree to work <u>with</u> us, not for us. If we commit an act that is considered an abuse of power by Spirit, many of our guides are likely to leave us. Any ally or guide that condones such an act, while it may be powerful, is also a guide that will demand sacrifice and significant donations of energy in return. Working with a guide demonstrates a commitment of trust. We trust our guide to be worthy to teach and help us. We must also trust that whatever our guide does without our direction is good -- just as our own guides trust us to behave with honor, integrity and good will. Above all else, you must learn to trust your own instinct.

For as long as there have been spiritual workers, there have also been those who would abuse the power. It is my very strong and personal belief that abuse of power is detrimental not only to those whom the person would seek to harm, but also to the shaman themselves. I've known more than my fair share of spiritual workers who have become addicted to the energy and power they work with, and lost sight of the fact that they are, above all, healers. Draining energy off other people might feel great for a while, but the energy belongs to someone else and so in the end the theft will have a detrimental effect. In the end, what we send out always comes back to us. It might return in the form of a karmic lesson, a drained energy body that manifests physical disease, a loss of guides, dreaming or even hope. It is my hope that through our introductory work to the elements, you will each learn the beauty and harmony of being in balance, how to energize yourself directly from Source, and how to realign yourself as needed, so that you can always walk the path with a heart, in line with your individual true soul purpose. It is my intention that the training you do with me will bring you all to higher levels of confidence and self-trust, so that you can dance through life as the empowered light-beings you really are, thus raising the vibration of all you meet, so that they can each do the same, and so on, and so on.

More Methods for Clearing and Warding

SMOKE – Using smoke to clear a space is a common tradition worldwide. Smoke, which is believe to carry prayers up to Spirit, is a sacred tool. It also helps get rid of nasty bugs, physical and spiritual. Use sage, rosemary, lavender, cedar, yerba santa, copal, mugwort, juniper, tinder conk, frankincense, myrrh, stick incense... these are just a few available options.

SALT – Salt can be placed around the perimeter of a space to create a boundary of protection. You can also sprinkle it through the space and then sweep it out of the house or vacuum it up (if you vacuum it, make sure you empty the vacuum outside the space you are clearing.)

WATER – Use sacred water or salt water to sprinkle, bless and clear the space. Holy water is good for this, and salt consecrates water.

FIRE – Connect with the fire element (more on this in the future), ask it to help you clear the space, bringing in light and consuming/transmuting any negative energy and walk through your space holding a flame.

SINGING BOWLS/BELLS – Singing bowls and bells are wonderful to carry around a space, clearing through the repetitive vibratory sounds.

PSALMS/CHANTS/PRAYERS – Many psalms and chants are specifically written to banish evil and protect the person saying them.

SYMBOLS/SACRED GEOMETRY – try drawing 5-pointed stars, reiki symbols, or crosses in the four cardinal directions to secure and protect the space.

STONES – place a stone in each direction, or talk with a crystal and ask it to create a perimeter of protection for you (make sure you ask permission, not all stone people are willing to do this.)

Suggested Activities

- Spend time in meditation or journeys to meet and bond with your guide(s)
- Journey into the Earth to meet Gaia

Chakras & Breathwork: An Introduction to Working with the Body

Before we go any further, it is important that we address the body, because a shaman does not work only in the realm of spirit. In order to fully integrate the teachings in this book, we must discuss how energy and spirit works in and through the body.

The word chakra is derived from ancient Sanskrit, and means, simply, a point of energy or power. The earth has chakras, the body has chakras, the universe has chakras. In our bodies, energy flows not just to and from the heart in the form of blood, but through and between our cells, in and around us, on sub-atomic levels. The body has many small power points, from the crown of the head to the palms of the hands and the tips of the toes. The largest chakras are known both by their location and by numbers denoting their order of ascent on the body. The higher upwards you travel, the higher the number of the chakra. For our purposes here, we will be focusing on the seven major chakras and their associations.

Chakras are often described as colorful, spinning "wheels of light." If your chakras are spinning well, they are "open", and you are healthy. When a chakra slows down or stops spinning, it is described as "closed" or "blocked". Energy in the body needs to flow clearly and regularly in a circuit. If part of the field is blocked, other places in the biofield will eventually suffer, much like the heart suffers when an artery is clogged. First, the chakras closest to the blockage will be affected, as well as the physical organs related to that chakra. Eventually, the entire system suffers. Our chakras help us gather, transform and utilize the energy around us. Source energy – the universal energy that flows through everything – and Sun Energy enter our bodies through our highest chakra, located at the top of our head. The chakras below that in our head and upper torso help step-down that energy so that our physical body can use it for cellular function lowering the pure source energy into physical energy that our body can work with.

First Chakra (Root Chakra) At the base of your spine, deep within your pelvic area, the root chakra is the center of your intent to live. It governs your immortality and fuels your ability to ground and collect energy from the Earth. Your root chakra is what keeps you safe, what shields you from disease and physical harm. When it is damaged, your life-force is endangered. It is primal, sexual, survival energy. It is associated with the colors red, black and brown, earthy tones. It affects the legs, bones, reproductive system, feet, and large intestine.

Second Chakra (Sacral Chakra) Here in your lower abdomen is your intent to feel with all the senses and levels of your being. This has to do with the connection you have to your family tribe or community and how secure or appreciated you feel. The more connected and sensitive you are, the better you may perceive imbalances in your non-physical self, and repair the problem before it manifests in the physical. It is associated with the color orange, and rules the lower back, genitals, hips and small intestine.

Third Chakra (Solar Chakra) In your solar plexus, your third chakra is the center of many people's energy and strength, involving your ability to protect yourself through the creation of positive boundaries. Issues of ego, fear and instability tend to land here, as this chakra relates to your personal power and ambitions. It is here that Joy is used to feed the soul, and so this chakra is associated with the color yellow. Indigestion is a common symptom of unbalance in the third chakra.

Fourth Chakra (Heart Chakra) In the middle of your chest at heart level is your fourth chakra, housing your intent to love and accessing unconditional love. Unconditional love manifests in the world as a compassionate flow of energy from your heart chakra. When this happens, love and compassion bless all of creation with the love from Spirit, and you are open to receive unconditional love yourself. This chakra is associated with both pink and green, pink for love and green for healing. Problems of the lungs and heart are symptoms of its imbalance.

In the past, the lower and upper chakras used to blend predominantly in the third chakra, and it was here that people would experience disconnection to their upper halves, but as humanity opens to unconditional love on mass levels, we are becoming centered in our heart chakras, and experiencing splits more and more in our throat chakra. These "splits" result from imbalances between our spirit, beliefs and ideals, and our physical, ego/earth-driven selves, and are best healed through the heart.

Fifth Chakra (Throat Chakra) Your fifth chakra is centered above your clavicle bone in your throat, and houses your intent to create, harnessing the flow of energy from Spirit and allowing you to manifest your dreams. If your will is not flowing, if you find you cannot speak or acknowledge your truth, your ability to dream and manifest is likewise impaired. The intent to create helps you bring your creative desires into physical being and is associated with clear, bright blue. Ley lines and energetic grids are most often seen as electric blue, too, when they are bringing in stable Source energy. Communication or informational related issues often manifest as sore throats or laryngitis, and can even affect the teeth and sinuses.

Sixth Chakra (Third-Eye Chakra) At your third eye, located about an inch above the bridge of your nose between your eyebrows, a few inches back in the middle of your brain, is your sixth chakra. Here is your intent to see. When you intend to See you see the true reality of the universe, and the illusions of mass consciousness fade away. You will see your way clearly, and things will tend to fall into place. It is associated with the color violet or indigo and blockages here can manifest as headaches, eye strain, sleep disturbances, or ear infections.

Seventh Chakra (Crown Chakra) Your seventh chakra is located in the crown of your head towards the back where your soft spot was as an infant, and is where you have the intent to receive wisdom and evolve. It is where you receive source energy and direction from your higher self and your biofield. When this center is impaired, it is more difficult to receive the correct information you need to maintain a high vibration and stay on the path of evolution. It is associated with the color white or gold, and is where you receive Ki or Chi from the universe. Crown chakra issues generally manifest as mental disturbances, confusing thoughts, and apathy.

The Aura and the Biofield

Your physical body is surrounded by the biofield, a larger energetic cocoon that creates and holds the manifestation of your physical body. Just as your physical body has organs, arteries and veins, your energy of your biofield flows in distinguishable patterns. In India, they describe this with the Tree of Life and Chakras. In China and Japan, energy flow works with the meridians. In Polarity therapy, there are oval fields, chakras, and energy currents. Everything works together to explain the way that energy flows through your body, keeping balance and maintaining optimum levels of health and energy.

The Meridians

Meridians are Qi pathways in the body. They allow the energy in your biofield to flow from organ to organ, muscle to muscle, in a regulated, cohesive manner. Each meridian, like any line, is made up of an infinite number of points. Many of these points refer to specific organs or places in your body – just as each meridian regulates the flow of energy in specific areas of the system. When a point is blocked, the qi becomes stagnant or blocked, and illness may present in the body. According to Traditional Chinese Medicine, gentle palpation of specific points can often initiate movement and flow. Likewise, specific herbs and remedies are used to awaken the energy.

There are 20 primary meridians and close to 650 acupuncture points used in traditional meridian therapies such as acupressure and acupuncture. Reflexology is a more accessible derivative of this science, and focuses on the points in the feet which have correspondences throughout the body.

Oval Fields, the Tree of Life and the Caduceus

The Tree of Life is well known throughout the world as a creation story. It is also used in Ayurveda and the Kabbalah to represent the human biofield. Source energy is pictured spiraling down the staff of life, the caduceus, from the top in mirror waves, winding back and forth like two snakes in an image that reminds many people of DNA.

At the top, or head, we have Source energy as it enters the body. The staff itself represents the energetic core of the body, the spinal cord and the Central Nervous System. It is the neutral core or pole of the body, and holds the blueprint for physical form. Where the energy begins in the head and aura, the poles are reversed, with the masculine on the left side and the feminine on the right. As it crosses down into the body, the right side of the body is generally considered masculine, while the left side is feminine. The right is positive, yang, stimulating, expansive, restless and conscious. Paternal issues tend to manifest on the right side of the body. The left side is negative, receiving, contractive, dreamy and yin. Maternal issues manifest here.

As the energy expands and flows downward in both its feminine and masculine, or negative and positive aspects, it crosses several times, forming the oval fields as it travels down through the body. Each of these fields is related to a different element, a different energy, and corresponds to a different element governing part of the creation of physical life. The oval fields are used to describe the quality of movement of energy through them, while the chakras refer to the quality of energy emanating from their centers.

The oval fields are easily found in the five main cavities in the body, the head (fire), throat (ether), the chest (air), abdomen (earth) and pelvis (water). The first oval field in the head governs thought, control and the fiery spark of creative direction. The second oval field in the throat has to do with the expression of spirit, sound and communication. The third oval field in the chest is about the movement of air in the body, circulation and life energy. The fourth oval field in the abdomen governs the functions of sustenance, assimilation, metabolism and the processing of nourishing matter in body. The fifth oval field in the pelvic bowl governs elimination and fluid activities in the body.

As with the chakras and meridians, if one oval field is blocked or malfunctioning other areas of the body will also begin to suffer pain or dysfunction. Wherever the fields meet problems can most easily arise, stagnating energy and causing congestion.

Each of the aforementioned energy systems seek to describe one thing. Our biofield is alive. It is a complicated web of energy. No one part of our body is truly independent of another. Every cell works together with a group. The better our biofield is functioning, the healthier and happier we will feel. And the better we feel, the better life can be. Vibrational remedies target various aspects of the biofield so that energy can move and flow to where it's going.

What we do know, what has been proven through regular scientific method and observation, is that the body is energy and that this energy is measurable at a distance from the body. We know that our energy reacts with and affects the world around us. We know that not only does our body emit heat and sound through its electrical and physical activity, but ***measurable*** levels of light. We are all walking around giving off approximately 100 watts of infrared radiation, as well as hundreds of thousands of photons of every second – low-level light.

So can we really measure the aura? This thing called a biofield? Well, scientists have been using SQUID magnetometers for over 35 years to quantify the biomagnetic fields of humans. Scientists at MIT and other universities have verified that not only does each organ in the body emit a distinct, measurable field of energy, but also that energy healers and Qigong practitioners ***emit the full spectrum of frequencies needed for cellular repair from their hands*** when they are participating in active hands-on healing. Quantum physicists have seen that the mere act of a human observing an electron experiment from another room has an effect upon its outcome.

Scientists such as Reinhold Voll have measured the electrical status of meridians and acupuncture points and found that they do indeed have definite, measurable variations in frequency or flow. Furthermore, when an associated organ is debilitated or the person is in proximity to a harmful substance, biofeedback readings will drop significantly.

Breathing & Grounding Exercises

Breathing exercises help keep us focused on the present moment and make us more conscious of our bodies and physical reality. Although they are related to the air element, they are also inherently grounding and relaxing. Deep breathing calms the nervous system and relaxes the mind. It helps us stretch and relax the diaphragm, which allows us to deliver more oxygen to our cells and have a healthier body. Conscious breathing also has the benefit of stopping the mind, allowing us to remove ourselves from our thoughts and mind chatter - again, putting us in the present moment.

The Four-Fold Breath

Increases Breath Awareness and helps center and balance you. Always breathe to and from your diaphragm in meditation and breathing exercises. Out-Breathe may be performed as an audible "oooh" or "aaah". Practice for 5-10 minutes.

Breathe in for four counts. Hold for four counts.
Breathe out for four counts. Hold for four counts.

Variation:

When you breathe in, intend to collect all the energy of the universe on that breath. Intend that as the oxygen washes through every cell in your body it is clearing away the old, the tired, the tainted, and leaving only the new, the fresh, the awake. See the energy of the sun and the moon, the stars and the sky, washing through you, enlivening every fiber of your soul and your being.

When you breathe out, intend to release every last tired particle that was cleansed from your cells with that breath. See every old emotion that held you back and tied you to the past bursting out with that breath. Imagine your exhaled toxins and despairs falling gently to earth, where they become one with the humus, reborn and renewed, becoming new plants, and new air, which you can then breathe in on your next breath.

The Energy of Air

Air often goes unnoticed by many of us, despite the fact that it is so important to us for our minute-to-minute survival. Air is the element that connects our thoughts and minds, it is the natural element that directs our individual connection to mass consciousness, to the living, conscious earth matrix of all beings. In our body, it is centered in our chest and our lungs and affects our ability to expand and truly live, not just survive. It is the animating breath of life, our prana.

It is associated most often with the color yellow, the direction east, the sunrise and new beginnings. This is appropriate because Air tends to bring us new ideas. Air governs the mind, our motivation and intellect. When our air element is balanced, we feel free and easy. We flow with life in a relaxed yet productive way. If you are deficient in air you might feel tired or detached. Without air, it is difficult for us to move, physically and energetically. Your upper back will tighten and lock up, your chest will constrict and you will find it hard to feel motivated or connected to life. If you have an over-abundance of air, you might have too many idea and not know where to start, or you might feel rushed and be moving too quickly.

The best way to connect with the air element is through breath work or singing. Playing the flute or any other wind instrument, especially outside, is also very helpful. In the body, the air element is connected to the index finger and second toe – massaging either of these can activate and normalize the flow of air throughout the body.

On a warm day, you can try standing outside with very little clothing on and raising your arms to the winds. This exercise can be a very simple and effective way to begin feeling and connecting to the air spirits. Many people resonate with one specific directional wind. The North wind is cold, serious, honest and pure. The East wind comes most often as a playful breeze, young and easy. The South wind blows warm and comforting, but also full of passion and has a fiery temper. The West wind can be both wise and melancholy. If you are interested in working with the winds, get to know them personally and see who complements your personality the best, and who might be your best ally or teacher.

Smudging, of course, also connects us to the element of air, because smoke travels on the wind to carry our prayers to spirit. Says Mic-mac shaman and elder, Evan Pritchard:

"[Smudges like] the sweetgrass and cedar are not only medicine, they each embody the four elements. The earth womb they grew from, the water that nourished them, the sun-fire that enlivened them, and the air they breathe – all four elements. To burn them while smudging is to change them from a sleeping to an active state. The smoke embodies the prayers of the people as it rises to heaven."

Breathing Fire & Sky

Breath of Fire - Sit straight in yoga position and breathe through your nose using your diaphragm, 1-3 breaths per second. This increases fire energy in the body, benefits the central nervous system, improves digestion and liver function, increases lung capacity and helps the body burn more calories. Use with caution if you have high blood pressure.

Breath of the Sun – Much more sedate than the Breath of Fire, use this breath to gently boost solar, heating energy in the body, ie: when your energy levels are dropping, at the onset of illness or if you are feeling unmotivated. Extend your fingers on your left hand and use your left thumb to block off your left nostril so that you are breathing through your right nostril. Place your right hand on your right knee with thumb and forefinger making a circle and the rest of your fingers extended. Breathe slowly for 26 breaths.

Breath of the Moon - Use this breath to regulate feminine, cooling lunar energy in the body, to relax and calm yourself when you are feeling stressed or anxious. Extend your fingers on your right hand

and use your right thumb to block off your right nostril so that you are breathing through your left nostril. Place your left hand on your left knee with thumb and forefinger making a circle and the rest of your fingers extended. Breathe slowly for 26 breaths.

When you practice these breaths, it can be additionally beneficial to use one of the following mudras:

The Bhudi mudra balances your ether and earth elements, helping you connect your body and spirit. It is often used to enhance communication, intuition and psychic abilities. Touch the tips of your thumb and pinky together and extend the three middle fingers.

The Ahamkara mudra is also used to combat fear and is believed to raise self-confidence. Most westerners know it well as the "All OK" symbol. Bend your middle finger and place your thumb its second phalanx, keeping your other three fingers held straight up.

The Kubera mudra is called the "Make a Wish" mudra. Use this mudra with deep breathing exercise to center and align yourself to your soul purpose and desire, and then state your intentions or wishes several times out loud while you visualize their manifestation. Touch the tips of your thumb, index, and middle fingers together and tuck your ring finger and pinky your palm.

The Mukula, or Samana, mudra is used most often to instigate healing in the body. All five elements are brought together here to balance their energies and create harmony. With this mudra, energy takes form and creative energy can easily be directed to manifest with efficiency and purpose. Bring all five fingertips together and point upward for general meditation. In healing, place the fingertips of the part of the body that is needing healing or relief.

Note: It is generally best to choose only one of these breaths to work with on any given day.

Standing Postures & Exercises that work with Air

Bear Posture: Stand in a natural stance (also called Paleolithic Posture) with bent knees, arms down and fingers extended. Then place your palms or fists on your lower abdomen. This posture encourages mental quiet and improves breathing.

Shaman's Pose: Start in Paleolithic Posture, then raise one hand with fingers up to the sky. This connects you to Earth and Sky (Air). It is grounding while it opens the crown chakra to source energy, and it also may be used to balance male and female energy.

Cliffhanger Exercise. Do this at a desk or table. Stand with your back to the desk or table and place your hands on the edge of the desk. Bend your knees and sink your bottom towards the floor so that your hands bear the weight of your body and your shoulders come near each other. Hold this position for 10-60 seconds without straining. This opens your chest and allows air to flow more easily.

Foods to help you connect with Air

Anything that grows tall, 6 or more feet above the ground – including most nuts and fruits. Birds are also connected with the air, of course, as well as many green or blue foods.

Items to connect you with the air

Blue stones, pumice and fulgurite. Wind Instruments. Bird or Spider-related items. Fans. Tree Nuts and Leaves. Sword or Athame (used in Tarot / Paganism / Wicca). Incense Smoke.

Suggested Activities

- Journey for Clearing & Relaxation
- Journey up the Tree of Life to meet an Air Guide for a message of Wisdom & Guidance
- Journey for a Song of Power
- Sing every day for 10 minutes

Fire that Moves Us

Here in the Northern Hemisphere, fire comes to us from the south as both a creative and destructive element. It is a transmuting element, changing the form of everything it touches. Fire is a good element to work with when you are trying to add energy or power to your spiritual work. Candles are used in religious rituals worldwide for this very reason. They light a spark against the dark, so that we may clearly see the way. In northern cultures especially, the tribal fire-keeper was always respected and trusted, someone with authority and power. They made sure there was always an ember available to kindle other fires, so that no one in the tribe would ever be cold or lack a cooking fire. They were friends with the air spirits and the plants, because a good fire required knowledge of what to burn and how to safely feed the fire.

Fire can be used to purify and destroy, to create life or give light. It is often associated with sexual energy and the power of the Great Spirit.

In the body, fire manifests as Qi and Kundalini energy, where its warmth and strength creates movement and stimulation. Without fire, we cannot move and eliminate food waste. Fire creates action and impulse in the mind. Fiery people are quick to act and react, full of energy, and generally dashing about from activity to activity. "She's on fire" or "they're fired up" are phrases we are familiar with. When fire is unbalanced, anger can flare ("he's got a fiery personality" can be a nice way of saying that someone is quick to anger). Not surprisingly, on the hands and feet, fire rules the middle digit.

What should we do when fire flares? If you suppress it and ignore it, you will create a dormant anger, much like a volcano, that creates toxicity in the body and in relationships. When it finally blows, you'll feel depleted and guilty, suddenly devoid of fire and energy. So what to do? Allow it to be. Express it physically with exercise or a safe activity. Write it down. Talk it out. Let it out gently and freely, but not by acting in a fiery, impulsive way. Remember that we need fire. Fire is Sun energy – without it our body goes cold and locks up. Our emotions can become too watery or heavy. Fire helps lighten the load, when used and expressed properly. It gives us the energy we need to birth the reality we conceive of.

Fire is associated with the gods of the forge, Brigid, Vulcan and Hephaestus; Vesta and the Kitchen God, gods of the hearth; and Pele, the Hawaiian volcano goddess. Also the sun, the lightning, the phoenix, dragon and snake – which brings us to kundalini energy. Kundalini is often referred to as the "fire serpent." It is a sleeping, dormant energy that in most people lies coiled at the base of the spine until it is awoken through spiritual work. Once activated, kundalini runs up and down the spine or central pole, through all the chakras up to the 8th chakra, just above our head above our crown chakra, raising both our physical and spiritual vibration. The activation of kundalini heightens spiritual awareness and allows us to receive more direct communication for Source and our higher selves. In some healing traditions, kundalini is also known as "body lightning" and it can feel like a tingle of electricity running up and down the body or a tremor in the tailbone or seat, as well as a cool or warm breeze across the palms and hands. Kundalini activation happens easily and naturally with meditation, breathe practice and even truly connected sexual union. It is one of the primary goals of yoga studies. Kundalini activation tends to result in feelings of pure love and bliss, a feeling of true-interconnectedness and deeper meditation.

Kundalini Activation Meditation

Close your eyes and take a deep breath in.
Breathe out.
Breathe in.
Breathe out.

Relax. Imagine you are surrounded by a huge glowing ball of light. The light is warm, pulsating. You feel safe and comfortable. Continue breathing deeply, in and out. With each breath in, see the ball contacting, getting smaller and more concentrated, as you draw the center of the ball into your body. See the ball centered in your root chakra, its boundaries getting close and closer to you, until it is finally a highly concentrated ball of energy residing deep within your body, in the base of your spine at your root.

Now see this ball of light, this ball of pure source energy, slowly uncoiling to take the form of a fiery serpent of light. You feel comfortable with the snake – it is your birthright, this snake, your body lightning, an old friend who has been with you, sleeping, all your life. Now see the snake begin to wind its way up your central pole, your spine, your central nervous system. It pauses at each chakra to awaken it with a flick of its tongue, as it travels slowly ever upwards. It awakens your first chakra. Your Tribal Center. Your Self-Confidence and Power. Your Heart Center. Your Center of Communication. Your Third Eye. Your

Crown Chakra. Your ability to access communication directly from Source and Your Higher Self.

Your fire serpent stretches lazily now from your tailbone up around your spine to rest its head above your own. You feel energized and awakened, full of excitement like a child. Your kundalini has been activated. Take a moment now to engage with your kundalini, with your fire serpent, and with your higher self, your soul, and ask how you can keep this energy activated on a regular basis and if there is anything you can do to better incorporate the energy into your body and daily life.

Now thank your higher self, your physical body and your kundalini.

Take a deep breath in, and a deep breath out. A deep breath in, and out.

Return.

Postures & Exercises that work with Fire

All forms are of physical exercise are good at increasing fire in the body.

HA! Airplane: Feet together, stand with your arms straight out sideways. Cross your arms in front of you 3 times, quickly, inhaling with each cross, then swing your arms back out, rise up on your toes with your chest out and exhale a loud "Ha!" Repeat 5-10 times.

Woodchopper – to release excess fire energy. Begin in Paleolithic stance. Put your arms straight above your head with your hands clasped. Take a deep breath and arch backwards, then exhale and bring your hands down between your legs, ending with a loud "Ha!" Repeat 3-10 times. Take your time, being careful not to become dizzy or strain your back with over-exuberance.

Ritual Use of Candles

Wherever there are candles in the world, they have been used in spiritual rituals. Candles create a wonderful focal point for meditative trance and prayer work, and, like smudge, can be used to carry our prayers, hopes and intentions heavenward as they burn. One may simply light a candle and say a prayer, leaving it on an altar or in a sacred temple space, or one can get a little more involved. If you really want to imbue your candle with your intention and will, a good method is to inscribe your candle with words or symbols of power. You might choose to use rune symbols, regular English words, magical alphabets, alchemical symbols. The added concentration of using an unfamiliar alphabet can help set your intention. After you have inscribed the candle with a small carving implement (a nail or toothpick can work very well) choose an oil to anoint the candle with. Anointing is an ancient method of purification and empowerment. When we baptize a baby with holy water, we are anointing. When Jesus's feet were washed and dabbed with spikenard oil, he become the anointed one (Christos literally means "The Anointed"). Choose an oil that speaks to you, you can even use a fancy olive oil, and rub your candle with it from the base upwards to "grow" its power. Traditional, multi-use oils for blessing and protection are spikenard, myrrh, frankincense, sandalwood, cedar, mugwort, juniper and sage. Once you have inscribed and/or anointed your candle, invoke your spiritual associates – power animals, guides, gods – state your intention and a prayer or blessing of thanks and appreciation. Intend to see you will done, as if it already has been done, and light your candle. Drum, smudge, pray, chant, meditate. Do as you will. When you feel you have finished, say another prayer of thanks and blessings for your spirit helpers and close the ritual.

Fire Ceremony

Fire is one of the most powerful, simple and accessible tools we have for transformation. Fire elementals hold amazing co-creative power. The simple act of calling them in as we write down what we wish to transmute or release, and then burning it, should not be underestimated. This act can be done with a candle, intending that as the candle burns down, the result manifests. Or it can be done with a larger fire, where wood is places with intention and layered with smudge, and the flames are called with intention, and the objects/written intentions burned are released.

A fire ceremony can be as simple or as complex as you wish. Writing out and then drawing your intention of the release and how you will grow from the release can be extremely cathartic. Burning representational objects can be healing. Speaking your intentions loudly and with feeling empowers your ritual – but you can also whisper it, or growl it. Many traditions actually encourage the development of a "ritual voice" which is more of a low guttural speech or husky whisper.

Fire ceremonies can be used to bring your desires to life, manifesting or releasing whatever you intend. They can be long and involved, or short and simple. Choose what you would like to invoke in your life, and write or choose a prayer or words that call in that energy. Inscribe your candle with the prayer or words, and anoint the candle with your fire oil. Create a sacred space to burn you candle, somewhere you can sit nearby for at least a portion of the burning time (the candle should take about 2 hours to burn.) Call in Spirit and your guides, and ask for their assistance in your prayers. State your intention, and light your candle. As it burns, your prayers will be sent to Spirit. Drum your prayers to spirit for as long as you like. When the candle has burned down, dispose of its remains in a sacred place, such as buried at the base of a tree or plant, in your own fireplace (returning fire to fire) or in a stream.

The Fire that does not consume:

There are tales from various spiritual leaders and shamans of an energizing, protective fire that does not burn. When you have developed a relationship with the Fire Spirits, it is possible to invoke them in fire ceremonies for protection or helpful energies. In order to show their presence, they might light your fire before you have a chance to; create a sudden, larger blaze; or even instigate a spontaneous combustion on or near your person which does not harm you and leaves your auric shield stronger and re-energized. *ALWAYS have water, dirt, or an extinguisher on hand when you are working with fire spirits!*

Foods to help you connect with Fire

Hot spices, onions, garlic, grains (ie: oats, rice, kasha).

Items to connect you with fire

Candles, Flames
Red stones (carnelian, jasper, red agate), Volcanic stones (lava, obsidian, pumice)
Thorny or spice plants, cactuses, red flowers, most seeds.
Essential Oils - Lemon, Peppermint, Ginger, Clove, Cinnamon or Sandalwood.
Stringed Instruments
Wooden staffs, wands, staves.

Suggested Activities

- Journey into the Cloud Realm with your Air Guide to collect lightning energy for rejuvenation and/or meet a thunderbeing/sky person.

- Journey to Gaia's great cave to experience her sacred healing fire.

- Journey to Pele, the Hawaiian Volcano Goddess.

- Perform a candle ritual or fire ceremony.

Flowing with the Water Element

These days we don't think about water as much as some of the other elements. Everyone is worried about the earth. Everyone thinks about air. But water makes up more of our body than any of the other 4 elements. We will die faster without water than without food, although our culture tends to be much more concerned with our hunger than our thirst. Our evolutionary migration out of Africa is believed to have been sparked by a drought, driving our ancestors out of the suddenly arid lands in search more plentiful sources of water and food. Until the modern era of large ships, water was the boundary of all land. People did not look at the seas and large rivers as areas of no consequence between communities and nations. They were (and are) the bulk of the earth. They contained the land within them. Even cultures that had boats, like the Phoenicians and the Vikings, still maintained a healthy fear of the water. The seas could be calm and gentle, then turn cold, stormy and unpredictable in a matter of minutes.

This is how the elemental spirits associated with water are, too. Some are lazy, relaxed. Some are capricious and dangerous. And still more water spirits have grown wary of the humans they once sought to teach – for wherever there are large communities of humans, water quality has always been an issue. These days it is even more of an issue, with huge cruise ships befouling the seas, oil spills and chemical discharges becoming a regular side effect of modern humanity.

While more transgressions are occurring, fewer shamans are around to intercede and work with the waters to heal their communities and the waterways. So the work we are doing is really important.

Water as an element in most healing traditions relates to emotion, sexuality, creativity, the processing and elimination of toxins and blood. In the chakras, it can be found most abundantly in the second chakra. It is generally associated with the color blue, as well as the color orange in some traditions (which makes sense when one remembers that the sacral chakra is generally orange.) Since the sun sets in the west and water relates to elimination and emotions, it is not surprising that in many traditions it, along with the underworld, is linked with the west, although in some East Coast tribes it is linked with the East.

If the water element is unbalanced, the person will be too! Too much water results in an overabundance of emotion, which can manifest with crying, sadness, or depression. Physically the person may manifest with water weight, fungal infections, reproductive issues, sweats or elimination problems.

Empathic people often have too much water going on, and really need to work on balancing this element. Too little water generally results in an overabundance of fire, making people feel brittle and over-stimulated.

A Water Meditation

I want you to relax and envision yourself by a body of water that you love. This might be a Caribbean sea, or a local lake, a small pond, a stream or a huge river. Just take some time to fully imagine yourself there. It can be any time of day you like, day or night, any sort of weather or temperature. See yourself there, perhaps seated comfortably, or maybe stretching in a yoga pose. You can hear the natural sounds around you of this place – the local birds, the breeze rustling in the plants, the water itself. Everything feels peaceful and serene, full of boundless energy. You are so happy to be here. This place always makes you feel so good. You place your hands on the earth and you kiss it. You raise your hands to the sky and you give thanks. You are so glad to be here. You feel wonderful.

We've come here today to ask for a guide and teacher to help you work with the water element. This guide will help you whenever you need to journey into a watery area of reality, it will help you swim swiftly through the underworld waterways, and teach you ways of healing and intuition. You begin to sing and dance at the water's edge, calling to your guide, singing it to you. As your guide approaches, you feel ever more joyful and excited, ready to learn. Relax now with your guide, who has much to show and tell you, and return when you are ready.

Foods that balance the water element

Food that grows from ground level to two feet (ie: melons, squashes), orange foods, fish, seaweed, water.

Water Animals

Frogs, Fish, Turtles, Whales, Dolphins, Crocodiles, Alligators, Hippos, Seastars, Octopus, Mermaids ;)

Ritual Bathing

Ritual baths aren't just about getting you clean (although they do). Ritual baths can be used to cleanse and prepare yourself for a larger ritual, or they can be the ritual themselves. You can use a ritual bath to focus your meditation technique, open your emotions or psychic abilities, cleanse your aura, really anything you want. Choose herbs or scents that are associated with your purpose (ie: cinnamon or mint for money, sandalwood for protection, lavender for healing or meditation, rose or ylang-ylang for love.) Light some candles. Add some salt to purify and bless the water. Place appropriate crystals in or around the water – some crystals don't do well in the water, so choose your stones with care. Before you get in, hold your hands over the water and imagine you are sending light and positive energy into the bath, as you bless the water (feel free to say a prayer here). Whatever your intent is, state it clearly as you enter the bath. Once you are in the bath, meditate and journey on your purpose. Stay in the bath as long as you feel connected to your stated intent. Once you are disconnected from the purpose of the ritual and you feel "done", thank your guides and whoever may have worked with you as a helper, and gather up your bathing items. Any herbs in the water should be gathered up respectfully with a sieve or slotted spoon and placed lovingly outside so they may return to the earth. Crystals that were used should be allowed to dry on their own, preferably in the light of the moon so they may recharge.

Oceans & Waterfalls

These watery places are natural ionizers and give off a TON of negative ions (tens of thousands, versus the hundreds you **may** be lucky enough to have in your home or at work). No need to even go in the water – just sit nearby and enjoy that neverending mist – you'll feel energized and clear, and you'll be taking negative ions in through your lungs and skin. What's the point? Well, negative ions boost energy, relieve stress and improve the mood (much like balancing the water element will).

Oceans have a particularly balancing and cleansing effect on the body, being so similar in chemical composition to amniotic fluid, connected with the push and pull of the moon, and charged with negative ions. When I go to the ocean, even when it is cold, I rejoice in charging in and submerging myself a few times. I find it extremely baptismal. Ocean waves upon the beach, thunderstorms and rapids also give off tremendous amounts of ions – it happens when the atoms break apart from the force of the movement. Even mountaintops have lots of negative ions, as the winds literally break upon the peaks.

Working with Water Elementals

Water elementals hold much knowledge about healing and spiritual work, and make fantastic teachers in these matters – if you can find a friendly one that is patient enough to work with a human! A lot of the water spirits can be flighty or grumpy, or even dangerous. Water spirits also tend to be chatty – with each other at least – and word gets around quickly when someone is a spiritual worker. Your reputation will precede you, always, with water spirits, and they don't usually let anyone get away with much. If you have wronged a waterway, the others will know about it. A good way to get on their good side is by picking up trash by the waterside, or even bringing them presents or offerings – just make sure you never put anything in the water that won't degrade naturally or benefit the waterlife there. They also like to be sung to.

Water from the Sky

Weather shamanism is an integral and ancient task of all shamans. As part of your job serving your community, there sometimes comes a time when you need to intercede on the behalf of your community (whether that is the land or the people) for a change in the weather. One of the most common problems that can face a landscape is a long period of drought. Droughts can create hardship for people, plants and animals. Sometimes they arise after a long period of cold and precipitation, where the combined wishing and yearning for fine weather creates an opposite effect of sun and dry skies. The weather spirits may very well believe they are doing the community a favor! And, also, sometimes the forests do yearn to go to their deaths in walls of flames, a death that many trees consider the most beautiful and heroic way to release life, leaving behind rich soils and new land for the next generation of forest. But, as I said, sometimes we need a little rain. Rain should never be called from a place of selfish longing or desire to play with the elements. Rainstorms can be powerful, dangerous things. Call them respect, treat them with thanks and wonder.

Most shamans in the dry southwestern states possessed rain kits, as did many European shamans where agriculture was a major concern. These kits would contain various rocks that held an affinity for various aspects of the storms. My own contains a large white quartz from a river to call the rain, a small dark gray and silver rock for lightning, a black stone for thunder, and a red stone for heart. The heart stone helps activate the other stones and represents my own desire for communal blessings. In general, I use only the rain and heart stones – together, these will call long, gentle soaking rains. With thunder and lightning, we get shorter, more powerful thunderstorms –

these may be used carefully if the community is in serious need of an energetic cleansing. It is best to call thunder and lightning during wetter conditions – call them during very dry weather and you may create a forest fire!

To make your rain kit, take as much time as you need to gather your stones. You may feel driven to gather additional stones for other types of rain or even snow. Gather whatever you need. Often, the best rain stones are found near lakes or rivers, already having an affinity for water. When you find a stone, sit with it and sing to it. Awaken the stone and ask if it would like to be an emissary for you to the rain spirits. If it agrees, you may bring it home. Once you have gathered your stones, find a high place to put them where they won't be disturbed (a roof or a tree stump can be good places). Gather some water from a waterfall, ocean waves, or rapids; wet the stones; and leave them there for a number of rain storms – some traditions say 5 or 7 for the directions, others say 9 for completion. Choose the number of storms that feels right to you and your stones. When they have gotten quite wet for the prescribed number of storms, bless them and wrap them in a soft cloth to be stored in a special pouch or box. When you need them, remove them from the box, make your offerings and ritual blessings to the weather spirits, formally and specifically state your request for the type of rain you are wanting for the community, and place the rock(s) back in a high spot so that they can call in the specified storm. Help awaken them again by pouring some water over them, again preferably waterfall or water of great movement, otherwise, make sure it is at least water which has been blessed. When the storm is over, thank the spirits and your rain kit, make offerings again, and put the kit back to sleep in its cloth.

Suggested Activities

- Journey to a body of water you love to meet a water spirit who will be your elemental guide for water.
- Journey with your water guide for emotional cleansing.
- Take a ritual bath.
- Make a rain kit.

Navigating Dream Worlds

Dreaming is inextricably connected to the lunar, watery aspects of our reality. All dreams take us deep into our true selves, allowing us to freely access non-physical reality without the constraints of this physical Earthly realm. As many cultures say, the dreaming world is the real world. Our waking reality is the myth, the place we need to wake up from so that we can see the whole truth, the bigger picture.

There are many sorts of dreams, but I believe that they are all, in their own way, truly real. I believe that when we dream our nonphysical selves, our souls, travel to other places and dimensions that exist both in and out of time. Sometimes we dream simply for fun or release, to work through troubles that plague us in our waking life. Sometimes we dream so that we can change our future. When I was pregnant with my second child my husband and I both had dreams about our daughter that were troubling. I had a very realistic birthing dream where she did not breath, she came out blue and could not be saved. The same night, my husband had a dream that he was walking with her toddler-self up some stairs at a baseball stadium, but then when looked down she was no longer there. She was gone. I knew that these dreams were signs, and being only three or four months pregnant there was time to do something about them. I did several journeys for my daughter to be sure her lungs would form properly and any karmic issues were being released – when she was born she was huge, healthy and alert, and remains so to this day. Sometimes, if we are given this type of dream, try to act on it, and it still happens as in the dream, then you can be assured that the dream was simply a sign from your higher self that this, too, was meant to be. You were forewarned so that you could mentally prepare, and know that you had done all you could do. No regrets. No what ifs.

And, sometimes we travel. Shamans in many traditions use the dreamtime to develop strong control over their etheric body, also known as their dreaming body or energetic body double. This body can travel over long distances and past time constraints to appear as a physical body in another place or time and do what is needed. A body like this may deliver a message or a healing, or simply give reassurance to the viewer. This is how people can be in two places at once.

Also, in dreaming many shamans and lightworkers are assigned some of their most important work. Some people teach people to fly or re-wire and upgrade brains or other organs. Some people perform healings on the earth. Some people work in the Akashic halls of records. A great many lightworkers are being enlisted in this century to help the planet ascend to a higher state of being. This is done in two ways – some lightworkers help perform "upgrades" so that individual humans can reach a higher vibration. Other lightworkers are working to clear the earth's atmosphere of old stagnant energy, which surrounds the earth both in our lower atmospheres and reaches far into the solar system away from our planet. This energy pollution is actually comprised of soul pieces that are stuck in their own illusions of reality – they have died, but they have not moved on. Some think they are in heaven. Some are down here as ghosts, some are little further out. Some are lost pieces of souls that scared away in traumatic events are hiding out until they feel safe to return to their larger soul. These souls are so stuck, some don't even know they are dead.

The things they all have in common is that none of them are reconnecting with the fullness of their entire soul, they aren't connecting with their soul groups between lives to regroup, learn and plan, they aren't reincarnating, and they aren't connecting with Source. The other thing they have in common is that they are ALL, every one of them, creating shroud around the earth that makes the atmosphere heavier and heavier, making it harder for other souls to move through it and move on, and making it hard for good energy to get through.

Many, many lightworkers are working all night while they sleep to remedy this situation. These people are truly letting in the light! They spend a lot of time with each soul, one-on-one, helping it get out of its own way, gently convincing it to move past the illusions it has created (whether they are beautiful or scary, the false realities these souls create are all illusions that hold back the soul), and move on to the next level of being. This, in turn, is allowing the earth to lift its vibration, and even helps our physical atmosphere improve. One group of souls (both incarnated and non-incarnated) who work on this are called the blue triangle people, or the purple triangle people, because they look like triangles or merkabas of blue or purple light, and you can call on them to clear spaces of entities and lost souls who need to move on.

Your Dreaming Practice

Dreaming connects us to the higher realms, because it is the higher realms. In dreaming you can literally do anything or be anywhere. As you practice honing your dreaming skills, you will have clearer and more vivid dreams. You will be able to distinguish between the real and unreal more easily, both when you are sleeping and waking. You will develop better shamanic skills.

There are three key steps to beginning your dream work:

The first step in becoming a better dreamer is to state your intent. Know and state that you want to have clear dreams that you remember.

Step two is to acquire a dream journal (you can use your journey journal for this if you like). Dream journals are invaluable for good dreaming practices. At the start of the night, write down what you intend to dream about, and that you also intend to remember it. Your intent might be to ask for guidance, or to travel somewhere, or for a message. Then go to sleep, saying your intent to yourself before you sleep.

Step three is when you wake up – immediately write down whatever you remember, even if it's just one word or a color. Don't make the mistake of thinking that because your dream is so clear you will remember it later after you shower. You probably won't. Write it down right away, with as little change in your position or lighting as possible.

If you practice these three things each night and morning, you will reach a point where you can remember an entire dream in detail, and eventually even all your dreams from each night. It might take a few days, a few weeks, or even months, but eventually it will happen.

A few other things that can be helpful in your dream records are to note down how you felt emotionally and physically when you woke from the dream, as well as to make a title for your dream that captures the essence of its theme. These practices can help you later when you try to decipher meaning, such as whether the dream was a way of working through your sub-conscious fears or if it was an actual warning.

Opening the Third Eye for Dreaming

A simple technique for opening the third eyes uses the breath. This is a wonderful technique to try just as you drift to sleep to enhance dreaming.

As you breathe in, pull the air in through your brow chakra to your third eye center in the pineal gland. As you breathe out, pull the air in through your zeel point at the base of your skull to your third eye center in the pineal gland. Continue this breathing, creating this tidal pull to your pineal gland, to your third eye, for 5-10 breaths.

Breathwork also has the added bonus of balancing the sympathetic and parasympathetic nervous systems, creating a calm, relaxed state that harmonizes mind and body. Elongating the breath out relaxes the parasympathetic nervous system, which is helpful to reach brain states conducive to dreaming and trancework, and elongating the breath in relaxes the sympathetic nervous system. While elongating the breath in and focusing on abdominal breathing benefits the sympathetic nervous system and regulates involuntary functions like blood pressure, heart rate, circulation, and digestion.

Entering the Dream

Shamanic journeying is a fantastic way to re-enter a dream. You can drum yourself back into your dream, or you can journey into someone else's. If the other person is with you, it can be very helpful to lie side by side with part of your bodies touching – foot to foot is good. The dreamer begins by sharing as many details of the dream as they can and saying what they would like to have clarified or resolved. Their partner, a dream-helper or dream-tracker, then journeys for them or with them to seek a remedy. When the journey is complete, the experience may be given to the dreamer using shamanic breath into the body or a crystal, or simply shared vocally.

Lucid Dreaming

Lucid dreaming is another way to consciously work within a dream, and is a primary goal of many dreamworkers. When you are lucid dreaming, you are conscious within the dreamtime. You can affect the actions you take, rather than just watching things unfold. You can control what appears and what disappears. You can shape your dreamscape, you can shift reality. This is a very important skill for a shaman to have if they want to become a dreamwalker, or someone who travels to other places and realities with conscious intent through their dreams, much like shamanic journeying.

Some cultures believe that the world we experience is the dream, and what we experience when we sleep is the reality. I believe that both things are true – I believe that all worlds we experience, both waking and dreaming, are real. That they are all places we can visit, and that when we are dreaming we can do extraordinary things. We can visit other people astrally. We can enter another person's dreams to deliver a message or have a real heart-to-heart communication. There are accounts of shamans who have become so adept at their dreaming, that their astral projections, or *dreaming body*, can appear as a solid form and they can be in two places at once, doing healing work in one town while they have dinner with students in another. This is, of course, fairly advanced work. It's important to start small and begin at the first step – having a lucid dream on purpose.

You may have had some lucid dreaming moments already, times when you were dreaming and all of a sudden thought "hey, I'm dreaming!" and woke up or shifted the scene. Your goal as a shamanic lightworker is to be able to control the inception of these moments, so that you can lucid dream whenever you need to. We start, of course, with intent. Before you go to sleep, follow your dream practice of writing down and stating your intent. Write down in your dream journal "tonight I intend to be conscious and lucid while I am dreaming." As you lie down and drift off to sleep, say this to yourself several times. Do not be disappointed if it doesn't happen the first night. It might even take weeks or months. Once you have a lucid dream, it will be easier to have more.

The next step is to give yourself a specific goal of something you can control in your dream – my own teacher had me begin by looking at my hand, which seems like a small thing, but is actually a pretty big deal, because you aren't just controlling your dreamscape, you are interacting with your dream body and using your waking intent to do so. So write down in your dream journal "tonight I intend to look at my hand while I am dreaming," and repeat it to yourself a few times as you fall asleep. Once you have mastered this, you can begin intending to do specific dreamwork while you sleep. You might try visiting friends' dreams (with permission, of course) or doing journey work. Spend some time developing these skills, and learning to recognize your own dreamscape. Everyone's dreams look and feel a little different, and knowing what yours feel like can be a great boon to becoming lucid in them, and also help you know when you are someone else's unfamiliar territory.

Sharing Your Dreams

Dreaming is so important to all of us. We all dream, whether we remember the dreams or not. Most animals have been shown to dream. Dreaming is where our soul takes flight. So how can we understand our dreams better? A wonderful way to begin to understand the language of your dreams is to host a dream circle. Get a few friends together who like to dream, and meet every 4-6 weeks. Each person brings one dream with them to the circle, something they don't quite understand or maybe that bothered them a bit.

The most important thing to remember with dreams is that we each have our own dream lexicon that filters our thoughts and experiences. Colors mean different things to different people – gray might signify sadness, or maybe peace. Tornados might be exciting and energizing, or they might be terrifying. So you always have to figure out your own meanings. In a dream circle, the first person tells their dream. Then, everyone takes turns saying what the dream might mean to them if it were theirs. Or they might point out the conventional literary meaning of a symbol, or the spiritual significance of an image. Ideas which do not resonate with the dreamer are just as important as the ideas that do, because it helps the dreamer crystallize what the dream does and does not mean. Always remember that only the dreamer can say for certain what their dream might mean.

Suggested Activities

- Journey for a dream guardian to help you with your dreaming.
- Practice the third eye breathing technique each night before falling asleep.

Ether:
The Fifth Element

Ether is present in all spiritual traditions and goes by many names. Qi. Orenda. Spirit. Aether. Akasha. Source Energy. Quintessence. In the Wiccan tradition it is the shown at the top of the five-pointed star – it is the element that energizes and enlivens the other five. In most Native traditions it is at the center of the four directions, it is above and below us, within us and around us. In Eastern traditions it is everywhere, the animating, unifying principle of Qi or spirit that moves us all.

When ether is balanced in a person, they feel peaceful and confidence. They are connected to Source and their higher selves. Early indications of an ether imbalance include a lack of self-confidence; stress and anxiety; hearing and balance issues; vertigo; joint problems; introspection, depression or non-communication; a lack of boundaries or feeling hemmed in.

If ether is out of balance in the body, all other elements will suffer and decline. You'll be tired, and eventually quite sick as the elemental centers begin to shut down. Without ether, there is nothing. No life. No Spirit. No divinity. Nothing. Ether is indeed quintessential. It is the non-physical energy out of which all life and matter on earth spring forth. Think of ether as the quantum space between atoms and particles, the space that goes on forever, with no real physicality to it except that which we have all agreed to see and feel.

Foods associated with ether include blue foods like blueberries, and all things fresh or newly emerged, including sprouts and baby greens. Bitter foods traditionally stimulate ether.

Clearing Distortion in the Akashic Realm

The Akash is the etheric blueprint of all that has been or will ever be. It contains the memory of all living things, the history of all of Source, all of creation. It exists outside of physical reality, so it contains the records not only of your past and current lives, but also of your "future" lives. Each of us is part of the Akash. Each of us has our own Akashic "Record", or pieces of the Akash that pertain to us specifically. As shamans and dream workers, we can access the Akash to clear old karma, to shift our own energy, or even to perform healings on other people. Working with the Akash can show us what is really going on in a situation behind the scenes – such as when a relationship is compounded by old issues from other lifetimes.

When you heal something in the Akash, it shifts your energetic blueprint which creates a ripple effect in the physical world. Your health can shift, your life experience can shift. You can heal genetic issues too, things that have been passed down from generation to generation within your family or even your soul group.

Two archangels that work a lot with the Akashic records are Metatron and Sandalphon. You can ask either of them for assistance in your work with the records if you like. Metatron is known as the keeper of the Book of Life (the Akashic Record). As one of the only archangels who began first as a human, he cares deeply about the welfare and ascension of humanity. He watches, he waits, and when he is asked, he helps. In fact, when you work with sacred geometry, the cube is dubbed "Metatron's Cube" and is believed to contain all shapes ever created by God within it. The cube represents the flow of energy and creation of all patterns in the universe. The cube itself may be viewed as the Akash.

A Meditation with the Akash & Archangel Metatron

Breathe deeply. Feel your body filling up with light with each breathe in, and your lungs expelling darkness with each breath out.

You breathe in the light. You exhale the dark. Breathe in light. Breathe out dark.

In your mind's eye, see yourself as a beacon of light. Stand, and you are as a pillar of light, radiant, glowing, pure. Look before you, and see another, larger beacon of light approaching. The pillar glows a brilliant pink and green, white and gold, and moves to stand in front of you.

This is the Archangel Metatron. He has been watching you for some time, recording your good deeds for all time in your Akashic records, and he would like to work with you this evening in a more conscious manner. He would like you to vow, tonight, to become one of his earth angels: one of those beings of light and positive energy who shifts the world around them towards ever-more positive levels. In return, he will help you clear old negative patterns from your light body, patterns you have accumulated from lifetime to lifetime, what you call karma, he is going to clear that for you now, tonight, for all time.

To begin with, he is going to install a metatronic cube within your breastplate. This cube is going to work for all time to insure that you do not accumulate more negative energy in the future, and help clear away etheric debris from your vicinity. You will be clear and full of light forever. This work is a great healing. Do not be in fear. Now, Metatron will also place a second cube in your clavicle area, and third cube in your brow, to help you create light-communication and light-thinking. This is a second gift. The third gift is the clearing that he is going to perform now on your soul and on your Akash. Your records are going to be cleared. This is a gift of more magnitude than you can begin to imagine. You are all great lightworkers, you who are reading this now. Metatron has been waiting for this day, for your line of healers to come to him. Let the healing begin.

. . .

You are clear and healed. Relax, and know that all is well.

Now, you can also use the cubes that Metatron has installed within you to access your Akashic Records, or the record of anyone else, with clear understanding. It is a simple process.

Begin by breathing in, and breathing out. While you breathe in and out, imagine what it is you would like to know more about. Maybe you are wondering what is triggering a disagreement at home. Maybe you are wondering how you can clear away an old fear that you have. Whatever it is, set your intention.

Now, to access the Akash, I want you to begin by breathing out, and as you breathe out, imagine blue beam of light emerging from the cube in your forehead, pointing in front of you. See the light shining in a clear, bright beam. Then, see a second beam of light emerging from your clavicle. See it emerge more strongly and brightly with each breath out. Now, breathe a third and final beam out of light out of your heart chakra, from the third cube in your breastplate. See these three beams of light converge on a single point of light in front of you. This is the point where your intention was set, this is the point through which you may access the records.

See the point of light creating the image of yourself or the situation you wanted to examine before you. Here, you can access anything. Imagine the beams of light working light a movie projector, but you can move through and between the rays of light, right into the energy, to see whatever you want. With seeing and knowing, comes understanding. Once you have seen what the root of the issue is, it is already being cleared. Sharing the message with the records' owner brings healing and understanding. Sometimes, you might sense that a specific action can be taken to easily wipe the issue from the Akash.

Take some time now to work with your own intention, so see what is manifesting before you.

. . .

All is well. You are well. Draw your light back into you, thank Metatron and any other guides who helped you, and return.

Cords of Attachment

Your body and your aura are constantly interacting with the energy of the "external" world. You exchange energy with everything is that around you, whether you mean to or not. This is simply a matter of physics. All energy is connected and interactive. Connecting is part of the web of life. However, while we were designed to enjoy the ebb and flow of energy around us, we were also designed to receive our sustaining energy through our connection with Source and the Earth. As humanity has become further and further removed from Spirit, people have learned to soak up other sources of energy. Rather than connecting with Source, which will sustain us with pure, high vibration energy, many people mistake the joy of connection to other people for a good source of sustaining energy. It has become commonplace for humans to gather portions of their energy, their etheric energy, from other people. People do this with family, loved ones, friends, and even enemies. Energy exchanges can feel good, but they can also lead to co-dependence and power plays in relationships.

When we exchange energy with other people, sometimes we form cords of attachment. These cords might form on unintentionally, or on purpose. They are designed to allow energy to flow in either direction whether we are near the other person of not. The more energy that flows through the cord, the thicker it will be. Some connections are meant to be mutually beneficial, where we send love and light to each other on a regular basis. But in moments of weakness, people often use cords to send feelings of anger or resentment outwards, or to gather energy from others without ever sending energy back to them, draining the other person of their energy. When you hear the term "psychic vampire", this is what people are referring to.

There is no reason for any being to have cords of attachment. We have cords today because we have forgotten that we can be our own sources of energy, and that we do not need to steal energy from outside of ourselves to light up our bodies. This is what we have been taught by mass consciousness, and something that we need to unlearn.

A good process to sever a cord is to see it dissolving into pure light. See the spot where the cord was attached closing, healing, and glowing as brightly and strongly as the rest of you. Repeat this with all the cords, one by one, or all at once, whichever works better for you. While you work, see if you gather any information on the people or beings the cords connected you to, and what the cords carried. When you have finished, ask Spirit to work with the light bodies of those people, to return them to their pure selves. Forgive yourself for any cords you may have placed on others, and forgive those that placed cords on you.

Vow Releasing

Throughout our other lives, we have taken many vows, made many contracts, many of them without any sort of time limit on them. Since there is no such thing, really, as time, these vows can carry over from life to life. Vows of poverty, vows of chastity, vows of obedience, devotion, love, silence, self-sacrifice, suffering, retribution, humility, and so on. We may have vowed never, ever to do something again, or we may have vowed to never stop trying to do something else. We might have made a pact to get revenge, or an oath to never speak the truth again after burning for a crime we did not commit.

These vows we've made, they still matter. A part of us still remembers them, and may feel beholden to them still, even though they hold no bearing or benefit for our current life. These vows manifest their effects on our lives much like karma, except they affect our judgment, our desires and predilections. Some vows even have to do with old agreements that may have bound you to other entities who feed through cords of attachment.

Rather than live beholden to old vows and a subconscious fear or reluctance to break them, free yourself by releasing these vows.

To release your vows, create a sacred space and relax. Call in your guides and higher self.

Now state, with intention:

"I am one with my spark-of-god-self, my higher, greater self, with all my soul and the light of Source. With conscious intention, we completely release and sever each vow, contract, oath, pact and agreement we have or ever will make with our self or with others that does not serve our highest good. The lessons I have learned through these vows remain, but the obligations are now ended. All vows, pacts, and contracts made against me are also now revoked and the connections are severed. This is my will, so mote it be."

You can thank you guides now and release the space, or you might want to journey to your sacred healing place for further cleansing and clarity.

Suggested Activities

- Journey to remove Cords of Attachment.

The Sacred Hoop

Directions have always had a major role in every culture around the world, and medicine wheels or sacred hoops can be found in most indigenous, tribal communities. The medicine wheel is built like the compass, having a center with four cardinal arms, like spokes, which when connected form a wheel. It is not surprising that we have wound up with four primary directions. We ourselves are comprised of a right and a left, a front and a back. The medicine wheel is a compass not only for our external world, but also for our own internal reality. The cross is simply one more adaptation of this representation.

As we now know, each direction is linked with a different element, and a different sort of energy. The North is generally aligned with Earth energy, mountain energy. It is strong, grounding and wise. The East is associated with the rising sun, with fresh air, new beginnings and change. The South is fiery, full of passion and excitement. The West is where the sun sets, it brings completion and healing, connecting us to deep emotions and the water element. The center of the wheel is you, and you, of course, are Spirit. When you are balanced and connected, you are one with Spirit, you are one with everything. You are one with the wheel of life. Source energy flows easily through you and around you. You are one with your higher purpose and you can walk your true path, the one with a heart.

Medicine wheels vary widely between tribes and cultures. Some use different colors for different directions, some have up to 28 spokes (perhaps representing lunar cycles), and some are 75 feet across! In the Northern US, the most common wheel colors used are red, white, yellow and black. These four colors create a wheel that represents not only the four directions, but also the four tribes of humans on the earth as portrayed in most native American creation myths.

The Seven Sacred Directions

North – stone, winter, night, white, truth, wisdom, power

East – yellow, dawn, air, light, awareness, spring, beginnings

South – red, fire, day, trust, energy, summer, optimism, creativity

West – black, water, sunset, dreaming, emotions, fall, completion, forgiveness

Center – spirit, soul, magic, rainbows, power, present moment

Above – indigo, divine source energy, cosmos, space, time, star people

Below – green earth, fertility, subterranean, subconscious

The Good Red Road

At some point in your training you will probably hear people talk of walking the "Good Red Road". The Red Road takes you from youth and passion to wisdom and a return to Spirit. The Red Road is about physical living – red is blood, after all. When you walk the Good Red Road, you are in balance and harmonized with the world around you. You are considerate and compassionate. You are generous and acting for the highest good, including your own. There is also the "Blue Road" which is the road one walks when they have transitioned from physical life and returned to the ancestors to council the living.

"One may be of any race or of almost any religion and walk the Red Road. The Road is a path, away. It's full meaning is the way one acts, the methods one uses, and what directs one's doing. There is more to the Red Road then spoken word or written words on paper. It is behavior, attitude, a way of living, a way of "doing" with reverence – of walking strong yet softly, so as not to harm or disturb other life."
— John Redtail Freesoul

Creating a Sacred Hoop with Intent

Medicine Wheels can be made out of rocks on the ground or drawn on a piece of paper. The creation of a medicine wheel creates a space that is balanced and protected. On paper, it serves as a reminder to stay in balance. We can also create a medicine when using our intent. Stand in the center or your ceremonial space (or anywhere you are wanting to bless and protect) and face north. Raise both your arms to the sky or stand in shaman's pose and call to the North. (A very simple, standard call to the four directions is given below, feel free to elaborate and talk more to each direction. Spirit always enjoys the attention.) Wait until you feel Spirit enter your space, then turn East and repeat your call, then South, then West. If you are performing a ritual, remember to release and thank the quarters for their presence and power when you finish.

Calling the Quarters:

Hail to the Guardians and the Elementals of the North,
Ancient ones of Earth,
I call you to attend this circle,
Thank you for your presence here.

Hail to the Guardians and the Elementals of the East,
Ancient ones of Air,
I call you to attend this circle,
Thank you for your presence here.

Hail to the Guardians and the Elementals of the South,
Ancient ones of Fire,
I call you to attend this circle,
Thank you for your presence here.

Hail to the Guardians and the Elementals of the West,
Wise and Ancient ones of Water,
I call you to attend this circle,
Thank you for your presence here.

Releasing the Circle:

Hail to the Guardians and the Elementals of the North,
Ancient ones of Earth,
Thank you for your presence here,
Go in Power.

and so on, around the circle...

Isn't a Medicine Shield the Same as a Medicine Wheel?

No, no it's not! A medicine shield is just that, a power object intended to protect its owner. Tribal warriors each had their own medicine shield decorated with their own totems and talismans, blessed by their medicine people for battle. Medicine shields were considered powerful yet fragile objects– only the owner could touch them, sometimes even if they were wrapped, lest their medicine be disturbed. Medicine shields were also used to protect the home while hunters were away, or to drive away bad spirits and usher in healing energies. A medicine shield might incorporate the directions and principles of the sacred wheel in their decoration, or they might consist of one central image, depending upon their purpose. They might be made of hard, tough hide to repel hand weapons and arrows, or from simple sewn cloth and fur for ceremonial purposes. Every shield is a highly personal, individual experience.

For a powerful medicine shield that harnesses the power of the sacred hoop, journey to determine your personal power totems for each direction: North, East, South, West and Center. Create your shield from a hoop of natural wood covered with fabric or hide, painting the totems in their quarters. Hang in your sacred space for protection and empowerment!

Power Objects & Altars

What is an altar? Merriam Webster defines an altar as "a usually raised structure or place on which sacrifices are offered or incense is burned in worship." The etymological roots of the word itself are Latin from the *adolēre*, or to burn up. Altars are now, and always have been, the places where you send prayers up to the gods or Spirit. When a native American puts out their prayer bundles on a rock and light some sage, they are creating an altar. When we light a candle at church and begin to pray, we generally standing before some sort of a temple altar. When you lay out a crystal grid on a picture on your dresser on top of a photograph so you can send distance healing energy or reiki to a loved one, you are making an altar.

Why? Why do we do this? Altars help us focus our thoughts and make prayer more effective. When we decide what to place upon our altar, we are honing our intent. When we stand before our altar, we are creating a space where we feel our physical, personal thoughts can more easily interact with the non-physical, inter-personal consciousness of Spirit, of God, that is all around out. If when we pray or do spiritual work, it is like making a phone call to Spirit – then creating an altar is like picking up the phone and dialing the number. It helps to get the numbers and calling codes right, too, because it helps our prayer reach the correct place by focusing our thoughts and intent. Water objects will help with healing emotional issues or divination, whereas fire objects are good for empowerment, creating passion and clearing away obstacles. Earth objects are grounding and protective; Air objects help usher in fresh energy and new beginnings. Try to include objects from each element to bring balance and harmony. Personal objects can be especially powerful for work with specific people.

You can make your own special power bundles by keeping things that mean something special together in a pouch. Perhaps you had an amazing rebirth when you went spent a day at the ocean recently. Choosing a few small pebbles or shells to bring home and place in a pouch or bowl will remind you of the energy and insight you found spiritually that day, every time you look at them or place them on your altar. Many shamans keep little bundles from life-changing events, and they bring these bundles out for spirit-work when they need a little extra power behind them for the ritual.

Prayer bundles are used to express thanks or convey a blessing. They are generally made from small squares of cloth or leather, filled with tobacco, power plants, or little crystals, and tied with bright ribbons and feathers. They are then given to the person needing a lift, or hung where the blessing is needed. Prayer ties are similar in sentiment, simple ribbons or flags hung to show that the prayer has taken place. As the ribbons or flags deteriorate, the strands of fabric fly away on the wind, carrying prayers around the world to where they need to go.

Suggested Activities

- **Dream or journey for animals to represent the 5 directions for you, doing one dream or journey for each animal: North, East, South, West, Center.**

- **Journey for guidance and make a Medicine Shield**

- **Perform the Vow-Breaking Ritual.**

Sticks & Stones

Many herbalists believe that one needs look no further than one's back yard for herbs. The plants I most need always seem to find their way into my yard. Trees will literally mature practically overnight to become fruit bearing, rare plants will self-seed in my flower bed. Watch those weeds! They might be great for smudging, or just what you need to clear out some old energy patterns in your body. Until you notice them, they will proliferate – they want your attention!

The most ancient and traditional way to learn about edible and medicinal plants was not simply through trial and error. Our species would not have made it that way! Shamans have always gone straight to the source on this one – books and oral traditions are great, but the plants themselves are happy to be our teachers.

Take some time to sit and meditate with a plant, and ask it what it is good for. Use your eyes and your senses, too – many indigenous tribes use visual and tactile clues of the plant to help identify its medicinal properties – a red plant for blood issues, an eye-like flower to treat pink-eye. Once you have received your messages, there is no reason not to then go to your library of books or search the internet for relevant scientific and anecdotal data on the plant. It is better to be safe, and alive, than sorry. But begin with a clear and open mind, talk to your plants, and see what unfolds. This can be a wonderful validation of your intuitive and communicative abilities.

A wonderful exercise to try at home is to grow a power plant from seed or a cutting. Power plants tend to be the ones that are protective, or help us with dreaming or visions. But really any plant can be a power plant. Every plant has special medicine. Even poison ivy, who works with the old karma of unnecessary killing, has power. You might plant several power plants in a colony, one to gather seeds from, another for flowers, another for roots, another for perennial usage, etc., or you might plant just one. Nurture your plant through all its stages. Sit with it on a regular basis. Talk to it. Sing to it. As it grows, develop a relationship with your plant. When it reaches maturity, ask it about its usage, what it can teach you, or how it might heal or benefit the human body or spirit. Be open – you might learn new things about your plant in addition to what you might already know about it. Science doesn't know everything yet – every plant has multiple of chemical constituents that can interact in a myriad of ways with other plants and the body.

Plants are Our Friends

Not every shaman or healer uses plants in their practice, but it is a useful addition to the holistic treatment of the body. Plants are high energy, natural remedies straight from Mother Nature. Whether we smoke them, smudge them, ingest them or smell them, they have a myriad of uses in improving body, mind and spirit.

There are thousands of plants on this planet, and they all have various medicinal or nutritional properties. Some are very mild, working to gently cool or heat the body, while others stimulate the heart or help the liver regenerate. Some connect with angelic energies, and others release endorphins or relax the nervous system when they are smelled. Every culture has its own pharmacopoeia of herbs, just as every herbalist has his or her own favorite arsenal of herbs that they use most often.

Herbal Allies

I have chosen to list a few friendly herbal allies listed here based both on their usefulness and availability in the United States.

Burdock is a wonderful blood-cleansing herb that detoxifies the liver, blood, kidneys and entire lymphatic system. In China, it has long been used as the foremost detox herb, and to treat arthritis. In Western herbal medicine, it has a long history of being used to reduce inflammation in joints and muscles, and help lower fevers. Burdock is part of many herbal anti-cancer regimens due to its ability to remove environmental toxins from the body and encourage healthy bone marrow. It is a very gentle, safe herb to use long-term for such detoxifying purposes.

Used externally, burdock root benefits many skin conditions, from rashes and sores, to burns and minor wounds. Infused in oil and applied directly to the skin, burdock also has a reputation for its ability to re-grow and strengthen hair. Leaf poultices relieve skin irritations, sores, and tumors, and have good antiseptic properties.

Cat's Claw has been used by tribal herbalists for 2000 years to fight bacterial infections, and has been researched extensively here in the US since the 1970's in cancer, Alzheimer's and arthritis clinical trials. Cat's claw reboots the immune system to regulate white blood cell production and performance. Early studies indicate that cat's claw has positive effects on viral and parasitic infections such as Lyme Disease when used in conjunction with conventional therapies.

Cat's claw can be useful in treating chronic inflammatory conditions of the bowels, kidneys and bladder, especially when they stemmed originally from a bacterial infection. It inhibits harmful bacterial and fungal growth, while detoxifying the organs and encouraging the growth of beneficial bacteria. The alkaloids and quinic acid esters found in Cat's Claw are anti-inflammatory and useful in the treatment of various types of arthritis. Cat's Claw is extremely high in antioxidants which encourage healthy cell division and can accelerate DNA repair. The herb has been documented to cause certain cancers to go into remission in humans and animals, including leukemia, and is worth further investigation.

Note: Cat's claw has been used for centuries in the Amazon to prevent pregnancies and help women recover from childbirth, and is not recommended for use during pregnancy.

Cilantro is a powerful detoxifier that helps stimulate the body to release and eliminate heavy metals while improving digestion. Because of its antioxidant and anti-septic properties it has long been used to help the body heal itself. It is rich in vitamins A, B, C, K, calcium, iron, manganese, and potassium. The herb combats fungal infections and candida, and may be useful in weight loss regimens.

Dandelion has made its way from its original home in Greece around the entire globe, spreading the message that herbalism really isn't any further than your own back yard. Its Latin name, Taraxacum officinale, actually means "official cure of disorders."

Dandelion is a powerful detoxifier and tonic, and is primarily used to cleanse the blood, kidneys and liver as well as the entire digestive tract. Arthritis and rheumatism in animals often stems from improper digestion and blood acidity: dandelion is a natural remedy for all such ailments.

Because of its strong cleansing properties, dandelion will clear many skin rashes and allergies, many of which result from waste and environmental toxins building up in the bloodstream and lymphatic system. For this reason, dandelion is also a good herb to add to any formula designed to combat tumors or cysts. It is reputed to stimulate milk production in nursing animals, and is generally considered safe for all conditions. It can be used during pregnancy to provide many essential vitamins, including calcium and iron, and to alleviate constipation.

Eastern White Pine is an excellent whole body tonic used seasonally in the spring and fall to help the body gently detoxify. The pitch, or sap, is very antibacterial and was used in drawing salves and poultices by many tribes. Try combining the sap with honey, gently heating until melded, for a wonderful cough remedy. White Pine Bark is an old and trusted remedy for colds and flu. It loosens and expels phlegm from the respiratory tract, and it stimulates circulation, which may ward off colds and flu before they settle in. It Is the second best source of powerful antioxidants in nature (grapeseed is the first) making it ideal when combating free radicals, arteriosclerosis and strokes. It also contains 3-5 times the amount of vitamin C as orange juice, and large amounts of vitamin A.

Garlic can be used in any case where the body is in need of detoxification or cleansing. Throughout the world, garlic is known to ease a plethora of ailments, from a weak metabolism, bad circulation and joint pain, to intestinal worms, respiratory infections and fevers. It has been shown in recent studies to have pronounced anti-cancer and anti-tumor effects. It is used to regulate both high and low blood pressure, as well as help to lower cholesterol. Used externally, it is a fine antifungal and antiseptic treatment. This ancient food and medicine is valuable to relieve intestinal parasites, and possesses sufficient antibiotic strength to help treat severe infections.

Ginger is used extensively to calm digestive disorders, stimulating digestive enzymes and soothing the nervous system in that area of the body. Ginger is also used by many herbalists as a blood cleanser, and a general restorative tonic for the entire body, especially the circulatory system. It is believed to help heart disease and lower cholesterol. Scientific studies have shown that ginger is a potent anti-inflammatory rivaling most conventional over-the-counter remedies. Ginger also seems to benefit diabetes in rodent studies. Recently, it has gained attention as a potential cancer adjunct.

Mullein is found throughout the United States, and its leaves were used by Native Americans to alleviate a variety of lung ailments, from whooping cough and bronchitis, to pneumonia, asthma, and influenza; leaves were applied externally as wound dressings. Mullein has a very mild sedative effect; this combined with its ability to expel mucus and remedy coughs makes it an invaluable treatment for seasonal allergies and chronic coughs. For a well-rounded respiratory treatment for head and chest colds, combine mullein with stinging nettle. Mullein can also be used to treat pain associated with urination, and to help heal internal bleeding of the colon or diarrhea. Along with vitamin D and many B vitamins, Coumarin and Hesperidin are both found in Mullein, helping to strengthen veins and lending it a strong antioxidant effect. Mullein is also reputed to expel tapeworms. An infusion of the yellow flowers in olive oil are a noted pain-relief remedy for earache. Externally, a warm poultice or salve made from mullein steeped in apple-cider vinegar will help bruises, pains and aches fade away.

Nettle is one of the highest vegetable sources of iron and a wonderful full-body tonic. Nettle Seed in particular is gaining popularity throughout the western world as a kidney tonic after several promising clinical trials. It has been shown to increase kidney function and treat renal failure with great success by bringing down harmful creatinine levels. As a diuretic and tonic, it cleanses and calm the kidneys and urinary system while raising overall Qi, or energy.

Nettle leaf and root are quite useful in most respiratory ailments, expelling mucus and easing congestion in both the lungs and sinuses. Nettle is an effective antihistamine, its own gentle histamines attaching to the body's receptor sites and preventing stronger allergic reactions. Rich in iron and potassium, stinging nettle is well-known throughout Europe for its ability to purify and tone blood and the circulatory system. Furthermore, its energizing and anti-inflammatory properties also make stinging nettle a valuable ingredient in any joint or arthritis therapy, and it has long been used both internally as a tea and externally as a poultice by Native Americans in this capacity.

Stinging nettles are ideal taken daily as an infusion during pregnancy, providing many of the vital nutrients a woman needs. In particular, nettles are very high in vitamin K, which is very important for babies' proper growth and development.

Rosemary will produce a powerful liniment, heating and penetrating sore muscles and improving sluggish circulation. A few drops of Rosemary taken internally can also be used to increase over-all energy, alertness and memory while decreasing inflammation.

Thyme is extremely beneficial used in all manner of headaches, emotional disorders, and sinus troubles. It is a particularly valuable anti-inflammatory and mild pain-reliever for muscle and joint pains, and a general remedy for rheumatism. As it aids digestion and eases a variety of aches and pains, thyme can benefit almost any chronic discomfort.

Many species of thyme, each with different volatile oil contents, tannins, and flavonoids are used therapeutically to tonify internal organs and support the immune system. Thyme is a fine antiseptic tonic to treat respiratory problems, uterine buildup after birthing, and externally to treat spider and insect bites, thrush and other common fungal infections. Thyme was used throughout Europe in households as a favorite strewing herb, along with rosemary, sage and lavender. Scattered on the floor and walked upon, thyme's antiseptic properties discouraged disease while permeating the house with its gentle, pine-like fragrance; this is further enhanced by its insecticidal properties.

Note: Being an emmenagogue, thyme is not recommended for use during pregnancy.

Willow bark contains the glucoside salicin, that becomes salicylic acid, and is one of the original sources of aspirin, acetylsalicylic acid. In its herbal form, willow is a gentler, but often more effective therapy. As with aspirin, willow bark will reduce fevers, joint and muscle inflammation, and benefit the heart.

Yarrow is a great all-around herb, with cleansing and healing properties for the entire body, and is useful both internally and externally. Yarrow was among the first herbs brought to America by our early ancestors, who had no way of knowing it already existed here. Native Americans used yarrow to relieve chronic fatigue and weakness, as a wound dressing, and to stimulate circulation. Internally, yarrow will cleanse the blood and strengthen many body organs, including the lungs. It helps purge toxins from the blood and kidneys, as well as bacteria and viruses from the body, making it extremely useful in the treatment of any cold or flu, and most childhood illnesses. It stops excessive bleeding, inside and out: use it to lessen excessive menstruation, heal internal injuries, and relieve bruises. Externally, yarrow's ability to speed the clotting process makes it an ideal herb to heal all sorts of cuts and wounds. Simply make a tea or poultice of the dried herb or use fresh, slightly crushed, leaves and place directly on the wound to stem bleeding.

Working with Your Allies

Herbal **infusions** are made the same way as a cup of tea, except the herbs are allowed to steep longer in the water, creating a flavorful liquid that has been gently infused with all the medicinal and nutritional qualities of an herb. They can be used in a variety of ways. They can be drunk for medicinal or nutritive effect, used to cleanse wounds, or as part of your bathing routine. A rosemary infusion used as a rinse will make your hair shine and soothe tired muscles. Soak a cloth in a yarrow and calendula infusion and hold it against the skin to draw out infections.

To make an herbal infusion, bring water to a boil in a steel or glass pot, and then remove from the heat. (Aluminum and copper are both reactive metals and should not be used to prepare herbal solutions.) Add one tablespoon of dried herbs, or three tablespoons of fresh herbs, per cup of hot water. Cover and let steep for 13 - 15 minutes. The longer it steeps, the stronger it will be. Dried roots should steep a bit longer, 20 - 30 minutes. Strain the liquid before use through a cheesecloth or fine metal strainer. Let cool and use, or place in an airtight container to store in the refrigerator for 3 - 5 days.

Poultices are placed directly on the body to draw out infections and bring down swelling. Poultices can be made with fresh or dried herbs. First, place your herbs in a heat-resistant glass, ceramic or steel bowl. Next, bring a pot of water to a full boil (for open wound treatments, boil the water for a minimum of 15 minutes to kill any bacteria in the water, or use distilled water), and pour a small amount of the hot water over the herbs, soaking them until they are softened. Strain the herbs, saving the infused liquid as a brace for later treatment or to add to your drinking water, depending on what herbs you are using. When the softened herbs reach body-temperature, they are safe to put directly on the affected area. Use a sterile cloth bandage to keep the poultice in place.

A wonderful example of an herbal poultice is yarrow, which will stop bleeding, clean the wound and speed healing. In an emergency situation in the wild, healers will often fresh herbs can be chew or mash fresh herbs and placed on the wound.

Herbal **tinctures** are cold infusions of herbs that generally take two – six weeks to steep. They are one of the easiest ways to use herbs at home: simply add them to your tea or water as needed.

Instead of being infused in water, tinctures are made in vinegar, high-proof alcohol such as brandy or vodka, or vegetable glycerin. Which should you use? Each has its own benefits. Alcohol extracts the widest range of medicinal compounds and the resulting tincture has the longest shelf life, storing indefinitely. Apple cider vinegar has its own beneficial effects on the body, including helping reduce inflammation and encouraging cellular detox, but it may affect the rubber seal on dropper bottles and has a short shelf life, generally 2-5 years. Glycerin also has a shorter shelf life, but its sweet flavor is most appealing to children and helps makes medicinal tinctures more palatable.

To prepare a tincture, fill a glass jar ¼-1/3 with chopped, dried herbs or ½ -3/4 full with fresh herbs and top with vinegar. Close the jar and store in a cool, dark place for two to six weeks. The longer it infuses, the stronger the tincture will be. Woody stems and roots should be infused for the full six weeks in order to be sure you have extracted their full potency. When the tincture is ready, strain off the liquid, remove the herbs, and return the liquid to the jar. Store in a cool, dark place. 15-30 drops of a tincture is considered equivalent to one cup of a fresh herbal infusion, depending on the strength of your infusion.

Infused **oils** can be used directly on skin or added to custom salves or balms.

First, you begin with a carrier oil such as olive, apricot, almond, or grapeseed. There are several ways to infuse carrier oils. Either fresh or dried herbs may be used, although we prefer to use dried herbs because the water content of fresh herbs may lead to spoilage. If you do use fresh herbs, always make sure that they are clean and fully dried off before you infuse them.

The fastest way to infuse an oil is by heating the oil and herbs over the lowest heat on your stove for twenty minutes. Crock pots can also be used on low, infusing the oil for 3-6 hours. The warmth allows the herbal properties to seep into the oil quite quickly, making this an efficient method. However, heat also accelerates the breakdown process of oils, which will shorten their shelf life. When using this method, be sure you are use grapeseed or coconut oil which are both more stable when exposed to heat. You can also use the heat of the sun to infuse oils, by placing a jar filled with the herbs and the oil in a sunny window for several days. Olive oil is not suitable for heat infusion if you are planning on storing it for more than a week, although the life of any infused oil can be prolonged by adding one-half teaspoon of vitamin E or 5 drops of benzoin essential oil per cup of carrier oil.

Cold-infusion poses the least amount of stress to your carrier oil, and is easy to perform. Simply place the herbs is a glass jar, cover, and place in a dark cupboard at room temperature for 2-6 weeks. When the herbal infusion has reached the strength you desire, strain and store. An oil prepared by cold infusion will last for 6 to 24 months.

A **salve**, or **balm**, is a wax and oil based ointment that is great for wound treatments and skin conditioning. Solid and long-lasting, a salve is a convenient way to take herbal remedies on the road. In medieval times, wives would often make up a salve for their husbands to take into battle or on long voyages.

Salves are easy to make. You can use fresh or dried herbs, or essential oils, or all three in your salves. The simplest way to make a salve is to heat one part shaved beeswax in four parts carrier oil on the stove or in a microwave, just enough to melt the beeswax. The wax will melt best if you cut it into small pieces or use beeswax beads. Remove the mixture from the heat and stir it a few times. If you are using an herbal cold-infused carrier oil, then your job is done. If you are adding essential oils to the mixture, add them now and stir again. Pour the mixture into a suitable non-reactive container and let cool. It will harden as it cools, and store for 12-24 months, depending on what kind of oils you use. Oils such as coconut and shea both harden at lower temperatures, and can be used in place of beeswax to make a cold-weather salve (just be aware it will melt in summer heat!)

Adding a drop of benzoin essential oil or the oil from a 400 IU vitamin E oil capsule for every 4 ounces of salve will also prolong your salve's shelf life.

Our (Mostly) Invisible Allies

Nature Devas. Fairies. Nature Spirits. What are they, and how can you work them in a constructive way? These are the highly conscious being who reside on our planet in non-physical form. Some of them (fairies, gnomes, sprites) help nature do its thing, helping plants grow, protecting natural, wild spots. Some of them (devas, overlighting angels) are actually associated with the spirit of a particular plant family or area.

All of them tend to get excited when a new human is able to sense them—once you start talking to them you'll probably find it hard not to notice them. They are eager to co-create with us, to share their ideas and messages with us. They want nothing more than to help us help ourselves. They want only for the world to be harmonious and beautiful. They want all beings, all animals, plants, people, stones, everything on earth, to be in balance. Sometimes they might seem angry or proud, or a little wild and scary. That's nature!

Fairies and gnomes began as regular physical entities, much like us. They were slightly higher in vibration, slightly less physical, but they were here on earth.

Eventually, they progressed to a point where they were yearning to experience a less physical existence where they could work more with the energies of life, and less with its manifestation. More with the spiritual energies of love behind the plants, and less with the flowers or trees themselves. They reside now in a vastly different plane of existence, where all is energy, and physical rules as we know them do not apply. Having been of our physical realm, they can still connect with us when it is necessary or wanted, but they can also connect more easily with Source energy.

Devas create magic with the physical manifestations of the land and the earth. They are purely non-physical beings. They play with the wind and the trees, the skies and the waters. Devas are more intimately involved in the workings of the nature of the earth. Devas have also been called nature spirits, daikinis, sprites and sylphs over the years. Each location on the planet, every little stream, each field, each flower species, every breeze has its own deva, its own spirit, complete with its own independent personality and disposition.

Overlighting angels are the angelic beings that work specifically with the Earth itself. They are in a different business than the angels with whom we are most familiar – Michael, Raphael, Gabriel, Uriel. Those guys watch over humanity. Overlighting angels watch over Gaia. The overlighting angels are more removed from than devas. They watch, and they help channel energy to the areas they watch. They speak with the devas and fairies, and feel empathy for all living creatures in their area but they do not intervene on a physical level as much as the fae. They will and do help devas and humans clear negative energy from areas when they are called in, and they do help connect humanity to Source. But they do not shift the winds or the rains or the sun or make the plants grow swifter or taller. That is the work and the play of the devas, the cloud people and the fairies.

Every piece of earth has an overlighting angel. Some watch small areas of earth, and some watch very large pieces of earth. Most pieces of earth have several overlighting angels watching over them, at different levels, feeling different stages of connection and inter-personal connectedness. So, as your home or street has an overlighting angel, so does your city, and the general area of your state, and the area of your country, and also your entire country. The overlighting Angels often use different boundaries than our human maps, but you get the idea. Your entire planet has an overlighting angel called the Sun, and also the Moon.

Angels and fairies can be called upon to help better connect you to the earth or other elements of nature such as the sun, moon, plants or animals. They are particularly attuned to clearing spaces, large or small. Call on overlighting angels to clear geopathic stress, or energetic disturbances in mass consciousness. Devas are great for shutting down dark streams of negative energy on your property, negative vortexes or portals to other planes and dimensions. They are wonderful for helping re-energize ley lines which have become corrupted or disturbed.

Think about the size of space you want to clean, and then call in the appropriate nature spirit(s). Always ask them respectfully for their help. They do not appreciate being ordered around, but are eager to assist us in any way they can, so long as our motives and our intent are pure. Be as clear as you can about what you would like them to do, and within minutes, days or weeks, depending on the job you set them to, you will see marked improvements. Ask if there is anything you can do in return or addition to what they are doing: sometimes you may be asked to put a specific crystal somewhere, or plant a new flower. They may ask you to take a bath in saltwater, or you may hear nothing. Often, fairies respond with a request that you clear a particular area of trash or let a small portion of your land grow wild for a particular time. Even if you do not hear the fairies or the angels speak to you, trust that they are there, and they do hear your requests. If they do not ask you for anything in return, a heartfelt "Thank you" or a small offering are always appreciated when you are finished. Joyfully, lovingly, for their hearts are pure, they seek to help humanity heal itself and heal the planet around them. Remember to approach the devas with respect and love in your heart, and they will respond in kind.

Working with Stone People

Many indigenous creation legends tells us about the souls and personalities of rocks. The stone people were here before the plants, or root-people. They were here before the 4-leggeds and the bird people. They were here before us. They are the record-keepers. They have incredibly long memories, both geologic and historical. They know our histories. They know other histories from before we came to be. They move ever so slowly, but they hold exceptionally high vibrations and amounts of information. They can't come to us on our own, but they will work with the fairies and animals to be where we will find them – trout might carry a stone upstream, where raccoon gathers it and bring it to a fairy, who will then throw it at your feet, just before the moment you look down at your feet and think, hmm, what a nice rock, and stick it in your pocket. When you buy a stone, think about all the work it has done to be in just the right place, at the right time, so that it could make its way to you.

Crystals can be used singly or in groups. Once you catch the crystal "bug" you'll probably start to have them everywhere in your house. You can use a single stone to meditate with or hold while you sleep to enhance visions and dreaming. You can place them on the body to amplify the flow of energy between the chakras or meridians, or to heal a specific area or blockages. Different crystals have different uses, just like different families of herbs. And specific crystals (plants, too!) within each family have their own personality – just like you share many traits with your own relatives, but are also unique in personality. You can even use stones to enhance your drinking water. Make sure your chosen in non-toxic, rinse it and place it in your water bottle or jug to empower the water.

Crystal grids enhance the power of your intention. You can place crystals in a grid pattern, such as a circle or a sacred geometry symbol like a star or a cross, to amplify their energy or create a protective boundary. They are far more powerful than any one single crystal, as the energy of a group always adds up to more than the simple sum of its members. Use grids to send energy to others for long-distance healing, to broadcast your desires to the Universe or to increase the charging power of your essences. Grids can be used to create strong protective boundaries or to clear and charge simple items like your food. Place crystals in particular spots around your home to create a beneficial living grid.

Different crystal shapes can affect the way the power of the crystal works. When you use a totally raw, unshaped stone straight from the mine or picked up off the ground, you are working with the pure power of the stone, whatever that might be. Tumbled stones tend to have a gentler energy, and send their power out to whoever rubs them awake – they tend to go relatively dormant in the tumbling process, to rubbing them or talking to them to reawaken them is necessary.

Faceted or cut gemstones and crystal points have precisely directed, amplified energy that beams from their points or apexed faces. Crystal wands or rods are especially good for directing crystalline energy. Sometimes you will see wands that have one round end and one pointed end. The round end can be used to massage trigger points on the body and direct tension away from the away, while the pointy end can be used to direct the stone's energy to a specific point. Pyramids and obelisks (pointed standing towers) can be used to amplify and generate energy and are great for creating domes of protection or increased energy for manifestation, while crystal balls tend to emit a gentle energy in all directions.

Suggested Activities:

- Identify three "weeds" on your property that you are unfamiliar with. Why might they have appeared on your land? Journey and see. Follow up with research of the properties of each plant.

- Journey and connect to the fae community around your property and house. How can you work together to co-create a better life and environment for the highest good of you all?

Harmonizing with Sound

Sound brings us deep into the core of ourselves. Many channels and spiritual works say the same thing: everything is sound. In the beginning, there was the word. There was sound. Everything emanates from the original sound. All matter is vibrating energy. Quantum physics these days agrees – matter is nothing but vibrating waves and cycles of energy harmonizing to create reality. You are a collection of vibrations, a musical chord of vibrations. We, as a species, are just beginning to understand what that means. How can we change the world when we tap into sound? Can we heal the body? Can we shift our reality? Yes, yes, we can.

Let's start with the cells in the body. Science has found that bones and tissue will mend more rapidly when they are exposed to certain frequencies, or waves, of sound. This means that playing the right CD in a room with that sound frequency can literally help bones heal faster. Over 80% of people report relief from both acute and chronic pain with exposed to frequencies in the range between 50-150Hz, and muscles can be strengthened using frequencies in the 2-100Hz range. The **purr of cats** large and small has been found to span precisely these ranges – from 2-140Hz – validating the old-time superstition that having a cat in a barn will help horses heal faster, and explaining why cats usually purr when they are injured, not just when they are content. **Tuning forks** and **Singing**

Bowls can work similarly, and are marketed for each chakra or area of the body. They produce very strong air impulses around them when they are struck near the body, and it is believed that the sound waves carried strong healing vibrations that travels the meridians and reaches deep tissue. Many scientists and doctors also believe that each individual organism, each virus, each bacteria, also have unique corresponding frequencies that can destroy or heal them – this is called RIFE technology – and is used to treat a wide variety of illness throughout many hospitals in Eastern Europe and the Former Soviet Union.

Using sound to shift brain waves is another good way to promote specific states of consciousness and ease healing work. We all know that classical music helps the brain focus and engage in creative thinking patterns and problem solving. Some music makes us feel happy.

Some music can raise our energy or help us sleep. Why is that? Music – SOUND – can change your brain waves. The brain operates at a wide spectrum of frequencies at all times, but there is always a dominant wavelength depending on what you are doing. These brain waves are measurable by EEG readings and the five main ranges are known as Beta, Alpha, Theta, Delta and Gamma waves.

Gamma waves are the fastest at 40+ Hz. They indicate hyper-aware state of heightened perception and simultaneous thought processing. They are present during the flight or fight response, and are also found in people with better memories. Gamma waves help us see every minute detail. **Beta** waves are the dominant indicator of adult waking brain activity. They cycle 13-30 times per second and elicit logical thoughts and sense activation. **Alpha** waves register at 8 to 12 cycles per second and indicate a relaxed, intuitive mindset. It is the state most commonly sought during meditation. Studies show that students perform better and develop more interest in their studies when learning from an alpha state. **Theta** brain waves come in at 4 to 8 cycles per second and indicate deeper trance or dream states with an active unconscious. Theta and Alpha waves tend to be more prevalent in creative personalities and those with ADHD – what some call the DaVinci and Einstein types. **Delta** waves are the slowest at 0.5 to 4 cycles per second. It is the deepest form of relaxation without dreams.

In our normal waking states, humans operate at different states at different age ranges. This is significant, because as we've already shown the brain learns new behavior and gathers information more easily the slower it is cycling. Babies and toddlers brains operate almost exclusively in Delta waves.

Everything is new, and everything they see, hear, touch, taste or smell becomes instantly encoded in their brain for future recall. Between the ages of four and seven years, most children are operating in Theta states. They still learn very quickly, but their brains are a bit more discerning and filter out certain information if they don't want it. Primarily in the Alpha state, older children and young teenagers require an average of 21 repetitions to learn new behavior. After the age of 14 the brain waves stay primarily in the Beta range, and adults will need 1000 repetitions or more to learn new behaviors, unless they consciously put themselves into a slower brain cycle for learning. This is why affirmations, guided meditation, EFT, and hypnosis often produce such remarkable results. They repeat the message, often during lower cycle rates, over and over, until the brain finally understands that you want to encode this new behavior or idea into its patterns of belief.

Repetitive **chanting** and **drumming** are also effective techniques that still the mind and affect the brain. This is the key to why drumming has long been used throughout the world as a tool for entering trance states, especially for healing and grounding work.

Slower brain waves have been shown to induce greater healing ability within the body, which is part of why modern medicine uses medically-induced comas to help trauma victims heal. The deep sleep-state relieves the patient somewhat from the conscious effect of pain, while a body in Delta state will experience increased Human Growth hormone, DHEA and melatonin.

Music which incorporates **Monaural beats and Isochronic tones** are marketed extensively online, and allow the listener to easily synchronize with any brain wave state simply by putting on a CD. Robert Monroe's **binaural beats** are marketed under the name "Hemi-Sync" and benefit from decades of research at the Monroe Institute. They are also some of the most pleasant to listen to, but they do require headphones for listening.

The Voice

Your voice is not just for talking and singing. It is one of your greatest tools for self-expression. It belongs to the body, but the mind almost controls what it is and isn't allowed to say. When a person begins to experience 5th chakra (throat, sinus and respiration) problems, we often ask "What are you not saying or admitting? What are you holding in? What are you holding back?" But the truth is that we are always holding something back. We don't allow ourselves to whoop and holler, coo and cry, the way we did when we were young. And the power of our voice goes unheard, unused. Toning, singing and chanting are ways to get back in touch with that, back in touch with our body, back in touch with our true selves.

Toning is simple. Start by groaning and moaning, your deepest, lowest, most primal sounds. Let them come out as they want, soft and low, loud and hard, for as long as they want. The voice, at some point, will begin to naturally rise, to naturally soften. A sigh is often heard at this point – the time when the voice gives into to its joy at having been released, at having permission to express itself. It might begin to chant particular sounds, it might begin to hold a higher pitched tone, just let it come. The lower tones are a release, they let go of old energy. The higher tones begin to bring healing, they bless and restore, they activate and align. They are, literally, higher vibrations. Pay attention to your body while you tone, see where the different sounds resonate, what makes you feel more energized, what feels uncomfortable or strange. Toning helps break through blockages in the body – pay attention to the area and the related chakra to see what sort of emotional issues or old patterns you might be clearing out (ie: the lungs might relate to grief or anger, legs to support or feeling stuck, pelvis to survival issues or sexuality)

Toning can be used to heal over long distances (sound waves go on forever) or in person. It can be used to charge and activate items for holy, sacred usage. It can be used to raise your vibration. Many people, once they start toning, do it every day. The shower or the car are great places for this.

Specific Syllables

AH – believed by the majority of spiritual systems, including Tibetan Buddhism and Hebrew Kabbalah, to be the first sound, the word that created the world. It invokes the seed of Spirit and creation. The Ah in amen, literally invoking the idea "So Be It." It is a compassionate, comforting sound connected to the heart chakra. It is the first sound we make when we are born as we breath in, and the sound we make on our last, final breath.

OM or AUM – In Sanskrit this is the sound of Spirit, the sound that birthed the universe. It is the first primordial vibration, the sound of creation and birth. It resonates within the diaphragm and solar plexus.

HU, YOU or OO - is another seed sound, believed by the Sufis and various yoga traditions to be the sound of creation. Chanting this sound is believed to lead to enlightenment and ascension. It can connect well to both the throat chakra and the root chakra.

EE – is energizing and awakening. It opens the third eye chakra and cleanses the pineal gland.

Transfigurational Toning

Transfigurational Toning uses the combination of the voice, spiritual light and focused intent to empower, bless, cleanse or awaken an object (or person!). call up your intention, see yourself filling with the light of source pouring through your crown chakra and flowing through you, and then blasting out through your mouth with your voice, fueled by your intent and your love, by spirit and light. Your fifth chakra is all about creative potential and communication – this is what it is made for. You can use a specific tone to resonate with a certain chakra, or simply focus your intention and allow your voice express your will however it deems best – that's right, just let the sound come and flow as it wants. When the voice ends its song or tone, the work is done. You can transmute toxic water into clean, blessed water this way. The most important thing, as always, is your intent and your will. If you **know** that the water is clean, then it is. You assign the identity to the object. You define your reality. This is a cornerstone of the creative process taught to us by elementals and Spirit. What you believe, you will perceive. As in field of dreams – "if you build it, they will come." You must focus your intention in a way that you simply believe and expect that which you are willing into being, and it will become that very thing.

Suggested Activities:

- Journey to ask for a song that will help you focus – a personal mantra or chant.

- Journey to the element that will most balance and empower you. Ask for a song or chant to help you work with that element

- Journey for a song of Healing.

Healing the Soul

Our being is made of various components and layers. We have a physical body with energetic, etheric and astral layers. We have a dreaming body which is created from aspects of the astral and etheric layers. And we have a soul, the higher aspect of us that remains ever connected to Source, to God, that helps create our reality and also returns to Source when our physical body dies. Many shamanic traditions see this soul as having various parts or layers, just like our physical body. A part of our soul that governs our genes and physical body. A part of our soul which animates us and remains connected to source. A part of our soul that is our ego or personality. It can begin to seem pretty complicated, but when you remember that we are all ONE and all connected and all part of Source, then really it all becomes semantics. Understand that there are bits and pieces, but also understand that you do not need to completely understand the complexities of our existence – indeed, there are not enough active words or neurons in our current experience here on earth to do so.

When we incarnate, the majority of our soul remain connected to source, and we "step down" a small percentage of our source energy to incarnate here on earth. Many mystics estimate that we bring only 5-15 percent of our soul with us here into our body (much like the small percentage of our brain which we use). The rest stays with Source, learning with our soul group and other teachers, overseeing our existence here and trying to offer up guidance through our dreams, thoughts and emotions. Sometimes, another small piece of the soul will incarnate into a parallel lifetime in another body. The more soul you bring with you, the more energized and connected you will be to your "greater self" or "oversoul" or "spark-of-god-self" Sometimes, the lifetime planned is so high-energy that multiple souls will incarnate into the body at once – this is why so many people remember being certain high-vibration people, like Mary Magdalene, Jesus and Cleopatra. These people often have anywhere from 5-40 souls incarnated together, to fuel them with more energy and ideas and in turn fuel the ascension of more people around them.

When a person experiences a emotional, mental, or physical shock or traumatic event, part or all of soul can be jarred out of the body for a moment, and sometimes part of it will refuse to return to an existence that felt so scary or uncomfortable. You can tell this has happened when someone is in shock, or if someone is exhibiting signs of dissociative behavior. PTSD, depression, apathy, chronic disease, and addiction are all common signs. If a person says they haven't been well or felt like themselves since something happened, chances are they've lost a piece of their soul. However, many soul losses can also go unnoticed, such as with pieces disappearing in childhood simply resulting in a quieter, more "well-behaved" child, or an adult that becomes just a little less fun or joy-full.

When a soul piece is lost during a traumatic time it flies off without guidance to find a "safe" place away from the rest of the incarnated soul, but in its flight it generally becomes prey to the fear which sent it running and does not actually reach a safe place. Often, it will create a small corner of reality that is fear-based and negative and keeps it hostage. Other times, it will create a fantasy-based realm of comfort to hide it. Either way, it becomes trapped in its own delusion and it cannot return until the rest of the soul has the energy to come and retrieve it. Unfortunately, this also often happens with entire souls when they pass on, much like in the Robin Williams movie "What Dreams May Come". All these delusional realities exist like an atmospheric cocoon around the earth, lowering its vibration and contributing to both energetic and real atmospheric pollution, making it harder for humanity and the Earth itself to evolve.

The need for soul retrievals is extremely relevant to your reality, and a good service to others. When you perform a soul retrieval to return a piece to its soul, or you help a passed on soul move on and return to Source, the delusional reality created by the soul piece collapses and that energy is released as well. Distortions within the soul-patterning and DNA of the client are reduced. The atmosphere of Earth lightens, making it easier for souls to return to Source on their own, and the vibration of the entire planet is raised. Each soul piece that is returned helps the over-soul release karma-based reincarnation patterns, and eases the way for the client to have to a more purposeful, joy-based existence on Earth.

To do a soul retrieval properly, you must work in tandem with your own guides, and be fear-less of the fear which has held the others hostage. Many traditional cultures looked at shamans who did soul retrieval work as "soul hunters" or "soul catchers" because they would enter non-physical reality with their powerful helpers to track and retrieve the souls. This work was seen lay-people as difficult and scary – indeed, many modern authors on the subject still view it that way.

Personally, I believe that soul retrievals are some of the most beautiful and interesting shamanic work you can do. There is no risk or danger to your own soul so long as you remain fear-less, for the reality you are entering is a delusion. There is nothing to fear but the fear itself, truly. Dark entities or animals which you encounter on a soul retrieval are simply the negative energy amalgamation, FEAR thought-forms created by the soul piece itself, which hold the soul-piece separate from the rest of itself. The frightened soul piece does not want to return to the place it fled, and so it does not. On a soul retrieval your job as a shaman is to seek out the soul piece and offer it warmth and comfort. Sometimes you can simply retrieve the soul piece, other times you might have to talk them into it and convince the piece that it is safe to return and that the client is ready now to embrace it and it will be taken better care of this time around. Often, a soul piece will have things it would like the person to do upon its arrival. A child piece might want to go to a fair, spend more time skipping and hopping, or have ice cream every week. A warrior piece might ask that the person learn karate, buy some tough looking boots or watch fun action flicks. A medicine woman piece might ask to have a certain tea every day for a 5 days or to burn candles of a certain scent. The client might have to wear more blue, or go out and have more fun. It is important that the client do whatever is asked, and take especially gentle care of themselves for several weeks while the soul piece re-integrates to ensure that it stays with the soul. It is important for the client to continue looking at their life and "doing the work" after the piece has returned, so that they can experience true, lasting, healing.

How do you find a soul piece?

When you are ready to do a soul retrieval, you can be in alone or in the client's company. If you are with the client, you should have them lie down and sit or lie down near them while you drum for both of you. Have the client close their eyes and relax. They might journey with you, or simply remain quiet and still. Begin drumming and call to your guides. State your intention to retrieve a piece of this person's soul, and ask them to take you there. The guides that are most suited for the journey will take you. Remember that you are part of source and just as connected to all of reality as your guides are – you all know, on some level, where to go. Follow the beat of the drum as your feet take you there. Once you find the soul piece, make it feel safe and let it know that it is time to return to your client. The piece may have built dark walls around itself, or projected frightening images that must be defeated before it will feel you are strong enough to safely see it home. Remember that these are simple thought forms, and that you, as an integrated soul piece, have nothing to fear. Some teachers talk about soul pieces that have been "taken hostage" or stolen by other people. This is not an accurate portrayal of anything that could happen, because soul pieces naturally resonate with their own soul and cannot actually be stolen or held hostage against their own will. Souls simply cannot be stolen in this way, because at their core all souls are part of source and are never truly disconnected – they only feel that way. So, even in a situation where the piece seems to have been held hostage, the "guards" are formed as projected thought-forms with the agreement of the soul piece.

Once you have found and retrieved the soul piece, there are different ways you can return it to the client, detailed in the following segment, Shamanic Returns and Gifting. If you are in doubt, ask the piece how it would like to return, or ask your guides. Whether the client is with you or not, it can be helpful to drum the soul piece home: the vibrations can help re-align the soul cluster together. When you have finished, you can share your messages and visions with your client, and your client might want to share their experience, too. Make sure the client understands the need for gentle nurturing and continued healing and care over the coming weeks, and pass on any requests from the soul piece. Remind the client that any unusual impulses or spontaneous thoughts that might arise will likely be from the soul piece, and should be honored in a positive fashion.

Shamanic Returns and Gifting

When you journey for another person, it is very common that you might find a gift or token to bring back for them. Perhaps a mountain guide hands you an edelweiss flower to give to your client, to bring purity and divine blessings into their life. Maybe you are bringing back their inner-child, a piece of their soul that ran away and splintered off from their body when they were young and scared. But how does one bring back a gift from non-physical reality? How can these gifts cross the divide? Is it even possible?

Yes, it is! Not only is it possible, but it's actually pretty simple. I'm going to give you three procedures here for returning gifts.

One of the easiest methods is to return the gift while you are still on the journey. This is achieved by calling on one the person's guides or power animals and asking them to take them the gift. This can be especially beneficial if it is something you think the person will need extra help or time accepting. Old soul pieces can often be more easily re-integrated when handed over this way, because the person's own guides will help them do it, which can allow both the person and the returning soul piece to feel more at ease during the process.

A very simple, conventional way to return a gift is through the use of Shaman's Breath, directed breath that is imbued with power and intent. Most often, the shaman's hands are cupped over the crown of the head, the heart chakra or between the shoulder blades, and the shaman blows the gift into her hands, throughout the energy and physical bodies. As she blows, the recalls the gift and visualizes it passing to the other person. The breath itself can vary from shaman to shaman, and instance to instance – it might be long, slow and soft, it might be quick and hard in several short bursts, or it might be tremulous and almost like a song. The breath itself can also be combined with transfigurational toning. Often, the shaman will receive instructions during the journey on where and how on the body the gift should be returned. If no instructions are given, follow you intuition.

Shaman's breath, toning and meditation can all be used to imbue an object with the gift as well. Often, a gift will ask to be returned to the person within a crystal. The crystal, upon connecting with the person, knows how and when to best release it to the receiver. This can be especially useful if one has journeyed for a loved one but does not feel they can openly share the contents of the experience with that person on a conscious level.

Preparing for Healing

Healing begins before a client even enters the room – you should make your workspace as blessed and protected as possible, using sage, meditation or drumming and calling in the directions and your spiritual helpers. If you like, light candles or place healing stones around the room. If you have to travel to someone else's space to perform healing work, make sure you prepare the space when you get there. Sage yourself and your client to help ensure that the only energy in the room is yours, that no one is bringing in outside vibrations that could disrupt the healing.

Before you begin healing work on a person, it is best to balance and smooth a person's aura, feeling blockages or imbalances that manifest in dis-ease by using your hands six to twelve inches from the body, stroking the person's aura in a smooth motion starting from the crown of the head and working down to the feet. This has a relaxing effect on the receiver and prepares her for further healing, while giving you information about what might be going on with your client.

The Healing Grid

All physical forms, including the human body, are created through an energetic matrix, also known as the etheric body. It can be viewed as a light grid, most often seen to be electric blue. When you do energy work on the body, it is this grid that most often needs to be repaired. If you have ever seen 3D animation videos of works in progress, this idea can be easily visualized – the gridwork looks much like a wireframe of the physical object, but instead of existing under the skin, the gridwork overlays the body.

Any disturbances in the etheric gridwork will result in imbalances in the physical body. Missing gridwork will result in damaged parts of the human body. You may or may not be able to see the etheric gridwork visually, but it can generally be sensed and repaired through journeywork or the shamanic state. It is this gridwork that cords tie into, and from which cords and other energetic implants need to be removed.

Harnessing the Power of the Rainbow

The Iris Healing Method™ is a form of light-energy healing that incorporates both hands-on and distance techniques. It combines well with all energy healing techniques, increasing healing on all levels. This method is an ancient human birthright. It comes to us through the Goddess of light, rainbows and communications, Iris.

The Iris Healing Method™ requires no specific training, merely the attunement which activates and amplifies your ability to generate the full spectrum of light outside our normal sight range within your healing session: the light and energy of the rainbow is focused by your hands to shine directly on the subject of healing.

I've found that this method gives an immense boost to regular reiki energies and augments essences with a noticeable rise in energy. It uses all light frequencies, every color ray, to heal all aspects of all levels of being. It works beyond all time, in all times, healing the past, the future, and above all, now. It is pure light, Source light, pure divine energy. It connects you to Source, to the God-spark in you, to all that is good and pure in you and the universe, physical and beyond.

Once you have been attuned, whenever you wish to use Iris Healing, simply envision a full spectrum light rainbow streaming in through your crown chakra and out through your hands as you direct the light out through your palms into the recipient's body. If you are doing a remote healing, you can imagine you are cupping a miniature version of that person between your palms as you project a sphere of the rainbow light around them, or you may stream the rainbow light into a photo or symbolic image of that person.

Create Your Own Healing Sanctuary

To begin this meditation, take a deep breath.

Breathe in. Breathe out.

In, and Out.

Today, you will experience a Temple that exists for you, through you. With each breath go deeper within your body, until you reach your inner point of stillness, the quiet darkness where creation begins.

Here, anything is possible. You are a god within your own body.

Now, in your mind's eye, turn to the North, and see yourself in nature. This can be your favorite place, or somewhere you have never been before. Here it is just you, and the Earth.

Visualize every piece of grass, every stone. See them clearly, vibrant and real. Breathe life into them, so you can touch them, experience them fully. Feel yourself in this space.

Here you will build your own place for healing. It can be large or small, with many rooms, or none at all. On this journey you will create every detail. This healing space will be a place you can return to again and again, for all time, to heal yourself and to heal others. It will belong to you. If you want, it can be a huge center for healing and learning complete with teachers and guides, or it can be a simple alter for healing in the woods, quiet and real. Here you can have seminars, learn any aspect of healing and evolution, and heal problems on the physical plane. You are the creator, and the builder of your healing temple. You may call your guides to help you, or you can do it alone.

Relax, enjoy your time in your healing sanctuary, and return when ready.

Suggested Activities:

- Visit your healing sanctuary and perform healings on yourself and others.

Healing is an Art

One of the hardest things, as a healer, is knowing how much work to do in one session. Every person is unique. Each healer has their own vibrational healing frequency, and each client is ready to receive a different amount on any given day.

If a large amount of clearing or shifting takes place in a session, it is possible for the client to experience what allopathic medicine describes as a Jarisch-Herxeimer reaction. Often shortened to a Herxeimer response, reaction or effect, or simply Herx, the term refers to the endotoxins released by organisms in the body as they are killed by a treatment, and is most commonly seen with the use of antibiotics or systemic anti-fungal treatments. As the microscopic organisms are killed and the patient begins to experience a massive "die off", the toxic gases and chemicals released by the tiny bodies creates discomfort when the toxins cannot be eliminated quickly enough. reaction is especially common during the initial treatment of Lyme disease, where patients will report that their symptoms get much worse for a week or so before they begin to improve.

Symptoms may include, but are not limited to:

Gas and bloating

Fatigue

Headache

Flu-like symptoms

Joint or Muscle Pain

General Inflammation

Depression

Anxiety

Fever or Chills

Diarrhea or vomiting

Irregular Heartbeat

No healer wants their patient to feel worse, so what is a healer to do? Before any healing work is ever done, the healer should "check in" with their patient and see what the upcoming session will entail. This can be done with a pendulum, through journey work or meditation, or through intuition. Before I meet with any client or conduct any class, I always walk around the room where I keep all my healing instruments and crystals. I gaze at each shelf and grab the pieces that speak to me, the ones who cry out "I want to come!" Sometimes I hear them as a voice next to me ear, other times I simply feel a small tugging in my heart when I look at a particular stone or feather. Checking in this way allows me to bring the correct tools for the healing, and gives me a heads up as to what the person will need to work on.

It is also helpful to have a set of questions that you ask your clients before you work on them, so that you can determine what state the client is already in and what sort of work they need. Have they been anxious and scattered? Too much air can do that, and they will benefit from grounding work. Are they constipated and a feeling frustrated? An abundance of fire can be eased with water-oriented healing. If your client arrives upset, simple aura strengthening and smoothing may be all they can handle for the day. If something big comes up, such as a spontaneous past life regression, you might ask their guides to slowly and subtly reintegrate the healing lesson for them, and refrain from talking about it with the client until another day when they feel better. When in doubt, always ask your guides what you should do next.

Once in a session, remember that it is often better to err on the side of too little work than on the side of too much. Too much work at once, and a very sensitive client may never return to get the full healing regimen they need. Too little work, however, will still always feel good, and allow the person time to process what they have received so that they can return confidently to receive more work. This is not to say that a healer should design their practice so that clients need to return indefinitely. That would be both unethical and unnecessary. Most of the best healers I know tend to work over a set number of sessions (often 3, 5 or 6) and they let their clients know how they intend to progress over the sessions before they begin working together. The amount of sessions within a "set" varies from healer to healer depending on their own energy frequency and healing methodology. If you are healing for pay, you might want to offer your preferred "set" at a discounted pre-paid rate.

It takes time and practice, combined with intuitive development, for a healer to know how much work to do in each session and who will need what work. Remain flexible, and pay attention to your inner voice. While you allow Source to work through you. Source energy is intelligent and needs no guidance. The less your ego is involved with your healing work and the more you "go with the flow", the better your sessions will go.

After the session, make sure you tell your client to drink more water for the next several days. If they say they already drink a lot of water, tell them to drink more. Drinking large amounts of water and eating lightly will help flush the toxins out of the body more quickly. Warm baths with Epsom and/or sea salts is also very helpful.

No one person is capable of healing all things and, sometimes, a healer and a client simply do not resonate. If you find that is the case or feel that you have done all you can for the client, have a list of fellow healers in various modalities that you can pick from to refer them to. Often, a person might need a little bodywork to open up more between a set of sessions, or a reiki treatment followed by some acupuncture or counseling. Do not be afraid to refer clients to other people.

Extractions

While you are working with the client's aura, or later during your energy work or your journeying, you might find discover foreign energy in the body or aura such as implants, harmful thought-forms, entities, or energy-draining cords – this is when you use a method of shamanic extraction or energetic removal. The idea of extraction can be found in almost every culture, from Catholic exorcism to Native medicine healers. As with all healing, the key is intent.

When you find something that feels cold, dark, muddy, heavy and/or foreign in the body, chances are it does not belong there. You may get a very clear image of what it is (perhaps a feather, a cord, a stunted looking gnome) and where it came from (a past life, a jealous co-worker, alien contact, genetic coding), or you may just get a fleeting, unpleasant impression of color or temperature. Follow your intuition. Use your hand(s) to give little energetic tugs on the implant, loosening it from the body, and then grasp it firmly with one or both hands and fling it firmly away with a flick of the wrist and/or fingers, away from both your energy body and that of your client. Visualize it being tossed in a blazing divine fire, or sending it to the outer rims of the universe, or sending it back to where it came from. Wherever you send it, it should understand that it cannot return. Some shamans cup their hand over the area and use their mouth to suck out the object, then "spit" it out into the fire. After you have extracted the offending energy, smooth the energy over the affected area with your hands and repeat the extraction process as many times as you feel necessary until all you feel in the area is clear, clean energy. You may decide to tell the client what you are doing while you are doing it, or after, or not at all. Again, use your judgement.

Group Work

Whenever a group works together with a single focus, the outcome is magnified. Studies over the last 40 years have definitively shown that there is group mind, a sort of telepathic connection that exists when people gather in one place. With spiritual or healing work, this mind connection offers tangible benefits. Imagine what can happen when you have a group of people all in one room together with the focused intention of healing one another or learning how to journey. Everyone who has joined the event wants to be there. Each individual in the group experiences a rise in their vibration, a boost from the excitement and intention of the other people involved.

Together, they form an intentional community where the sum is greater the parts involved. Meditative states are reached more easily with stronger results. Healing work is empowered and more targeted.

This natural tendency towards group mind can be further enhanced through close proximity or physical contact. Our outer edges of our auras (known in the scientific community as our biofield) naturally comingle when we are within 5-15 feet of another person. The closer we get, the more our energies connect on an etheric level, and if we touch we create an electromagnetic connection that resonates on all levels, including the physical. There are several ways to harness this energy. One way is to form a **train** where each person puts their hand(s) on the shoulder(s) of the person in front – the train may be linear or circular. Another way is to sit in a **circle holding hands**, with one facing hand up and one facing hand down. Groups can also **lie in a circle**, foot to upper arm, or heads on stomachs (the latter is a common group trust-building exercise, creating a lot of laughter and camaraderie.) **Spirit Canoes** can be formed with all the people lying down, side by side, foot to shoulder, with a drummer at the rudder. Groups can be split into **partners**, too, connecting foot to foot, head to head, or shoulder to shoulder. If one partner is drumming, the drummer may sit up cross-legged with the partner lying down in front of them with their head touching the drummer's calves.

Working with Children

Sometimes you might work with young people, or be asked how to a parent may raise a consciously awake child – keep them in touch with their innate divinity. The secret is to let the children be themselves. When you talk to them, speak to them like real people. They understand more than you think. They came in more awake, more enlightened, and are vibrating at a higher level of Source and they will find their own way naturally. Do not worry about what they want to do. Allow them to express themselves freely and they will tell you what they need. Provide a framework of knowledge and experiences so that they can find their own way, while you embrace them fully with love.

How to Use a Pendulum

Begin by visualizing yourself in a white circle or pyramid of light. Focus your intention on being fully protected and in a space where only light and love may enter in. "Program" your pendulum by declaring whose guidance is allowed to come through – are you connecting with your higher self, your guides, Source, the angels? Decide and declare your intentions before you begin. Once you are ready, hold the pendulum in your hand between your thumb and forefinger, or by hanging the string between your index and middle fingers. Ask the pendulum to show you what a "YES" answer looks like, and what a "NO" answer looks like. The movements should be different for each one, and the pendulum might swing in circle clockwise or counter-clockwise, from side to side or forward and backward. You should do this every time you use your pendulum, because sometimes the movements will change based on outside effects such as geographic location, solar flares, or a reversal in your own energy. Once you know your pendulums "vocabulary" for the day, you may begin asking yes and no questions. Frame your questions carefully. If you want to know if you "should" do something, it is best to ask something like "will it be in for the highest good of all involved if I.." "If I _____, is _____ most likely to happen." Pendulums tend to work for simple, direct questions. They can also be used to show if the energy in a place or on a person is flowing well – in healing work, using a pendulum over the chakras can tell you if an energy center is open, closed, or slightly blocked. The more open a chakra is, the stronger the pendulum will swing. If it is completely blocked, the pendulum will not move at all.

Honoring the Ancestors

There are many ancestors. In some cases, when we speak of ancestors, we mean "ALL our ancestors" which includes the stone people, the root tribes, the four-leggeds, and the sky people. When we speak of all our ancestors, we speak of all who have gone before us and held knowledge on this plane. We speak of all of creation, all of the souls and pieces of source with whom we are always, and will forever remain, inextricably entwined. Here, now, I speak of our closer ancestors – those with whom we share close DNA, those who have birthed us, and whom we have or will birthed. I speak of those who have come before and of our direct descendants.

When you work with the ancestors, with your direct genetic lineage, your brothers and sisters, mothers and uncles, grandfathers and daughters, you work to heal the DNA of you and your tribe. Anything that you heal in your own DNA becomes cleared from the DNA of your entire genetic lineage. A genetic pattern of bad knees or poverty can be cleared with a good day's work on the etheric plane. This can be done through energy work, shamanic journeying, dreamwork or the akashic records. There are many ways to access and assess DNA patterning and distortions. Once you identify the issues, they may be healed through vow-breaking rituals, gridwork healing and extractions, akashic clearing or soul retrieval, to name just a few methods you have learned. Sometimes, when you meet with the ancestors, they can have important messages for you from the higher realms, or things they think you need to work on for the good of your community or your tribe.

Always, treat those who appear to you from your tribe with honor and gratitude, even if this was someone you did not like when they were alive. Once a soul passes on to the other side, they are re-integrated with their entire soul cluster – they are no longer playing the part of the person who you remember. They might appear to you as that person, because they hold a piece of that memory fragment, but they are also part of All that Is, and no longer part of the dualistic good/evil judgment-based reality which we so enjoy here on Earth. Instead, they hold all the wisdom of their soul cluster, and can also fully access the entire accumulated knowledge and experience of their (and thus your) tribal DNA, as it has always been, and as it will someday become. Remember – there is no time, so here you can access information both from the future and from the past.

You can journey to your ancestors, or you can meditate. Below is a nice, gentle meditation you might use to meet your tribe of ancestors.

Settle in and get comfortable, close your eyes and relax. Imagine yourself at a comfortable outdoor gathering space. A small bonfire burns safely in the clearing. Hot cider and treats cover a table nearby, and your family stands nearby, enjoying the warmth and company. You see people who have passed on, ancestors from times long passed, and young children run around, descendants of your family lineage who have yet to be born.

Here is your genetic lineage, those who carry your DNA and share your same genetic patterning. Remember that when you clear old blockages and patterns from your DNA, they are cleared for everyone who is here with you, and many, many more. Do you have special messages for anyone here, or any questions you've been wanting to ask? Now is the perfect time. Enjoy these precious moments with your ancestors, and don't be afraid to ask for a healing. If there is music, join in the dancing and bring joy to your lineage. Take some time to enjoy the gathering.

Now return, time to thank your ancestors, hug whomever you have been talking to, and return to your body, back into this room, into your chair, and be thankful. Know that you can return to your ancestral gathering place whenever you wish. All is well. Return.

The Shamanic Lightworker's Toolkit

Most healers, be they working with the etheric energies or conventional medicines, have a toolkit. For an allopathic doctor, the toolkit is comprised of scientific reference journals, mentors, medicines, scalpels, thermometers, ECG machines, to name just a few things. Each medical specialty has its own specialized toolkit, in addition to the tools of the trade which all doctors acquire in medical school. Alternative healers have a little more freedom. Each shamanic lightworker will develop their own toolkit that best fits the modalities that they choose to incorporate within their healing work. There are many tools to choose from, including the following:

Sage and incense
Feathers
Drums, rattles, singing bowls, chimes
Chants, songs, toning
Meditation or trance work
Journeying
Medicinal or transformative plants, flowers and herbs
Medicine Bags, Prayer Ties
The Medicine Wheel
Guides (Angels, Animal, Goddesses, Gods, Elementals, Aliens, Ancestors)
Mudras, Physical Stances or Exercises
Dreamwork
Pendulums

Ceremonial Clothing

Crystals

Divinatory Techniques such as Tarot or Palm Reading

Colored Lamps, Candles

Prayer sticks, talking sticks, wands and staffs

Books, Magazines, Mentors, Peers

The toolkit comes together differently for each shamanic lightworker. You may use all the tools listed, and more. You might only use a few. Some, you might reserve for special need, while others you might use daily. Are any of the tools necessary? No. Each tool is simply something that can help hone your focus and increase your attention to your intention. **When one works with spirit, the most important tool you have is your intent.** Without focus, without intent, spirit remain undirected and uninvited. Intend to invite the magic of Spirit, the blessing of all-that-is into your life, and watch the magic unfold.

Dressing Up to Power Up

Every culture, both ancient and modern, dresses up for special events. Everyone does it for job interviews, to invite success. Worshippers don their best apparel before entering their temples or cathedrals, to show respect and acknowledge that when they are engaged in prayer on holy ground, it is something to celebrate. Most scriptures refer to the body as a temple – it should be maintained and respected, treated well, and dressed up!

When you engage in spirit work, putting on special ceremonial clothing and items that you only use when you engage in spirit work can be extremely helpful on many levels. First, and perhaps most importantly, wearing ceremonial clothing is a signal to your subconscious that you are entering another state and about to do something special. It is another tool that can greatly focus you intent. Second, each time you wear your ceremonial clothing it will become imbued with the heightened energy of your rituals and healing work. Just like a prayer uttered a thousand times by a thousand people begins to take on its own power and force, eventually the clothing itself becomes empowered by the work you do and will take on its own life-force and personality. Third, you can create or alter your clothing and accessories to have specific magical, mystical properties, and then awaken them with toning, drumming and ritual to birth them. You might make a special prayer shawl that you use to help signal your gratitude to your guides. You might have a shirt that you wear for protection when you travel to other world, or a special dreaming necklace. Masks are a special form of ceremonial wear that actually help shamans transform into other aspects of ourselves and of Source.

Any accessory or clothing can be made into a ceremonial object, but most traditions stress the use of natural materials whenever possible. Animal hides or skins should be gathered from ethical, humane sources whenever possible. Animal hides will imbue the object with the spirit and energy of that animal totem, and can be useful for protective items. Plant fibers have a lighter feel and tend to automatically lift ones vibration. Try to use organic and fair-trade items if you can. Different metals and stones have specific properties and can be used to further empower your items.

Before you work with any material, bless it and thank its original form for the gift it has made you. Call in the elements and whatever guides or gods you are wanting the item to be connected with, thank them all and ask for their blessings upon your item. If you are working with something that you found used, say at a tag sale or in someone's old barn, take extra time to really cleanse the item of any old energy and bless it, reassuring it all the while that it is loved, only light surrounds it and all is well now. Journeys and meditations can be used to ask for guidance on how and when the item should be made and activated. You might draw symbols on it, sew in beads, or dye it new colors. There might be bells for dancing with your power animals, or copper wire to improve your energy flow. Once the item is made, you should thank it again and bless it again, and state your intentions for the energies this item will carry for you, and how you plan to use it. When you let the universe know that you mean business, that you are serious about your work, the Universe repays you by taking you and your prayers seriously, too. You are a powerful, magical being in a mystical, magical world – claim your power and dress up to power up!

Is Light and Dark the Same as Good and Evil?

There are various kinds of shamanic work one can enter into. Not all shamans work the same way, or hold the same beliefs. This is good. Diversity of thought and function is what keeps humanity growing and evolving.

Shamans who work with the light work primarily as healers and community leaders. Plant medicine, energy healing, teaching, and ritual or journey work for the benefit of the community are all common examples of shamanic lightworking.

Shamans who work with the shadows perform soul retrievals and enter into the Akash for deep healing and release. They might remove curses, perform clearings, or engage in shapeshifting.

Shamans who work with the dark work are familiar with how to invoke power allies, dark spirits and demons, as well as with how to cast them out. These shamans know how to remove curses and perform exorcisms, and how to invoke the curses, too. Dark work can be dangerous and scary, especially for the uninitiated, and should not be entered into lightly.

Dark is not the same as malevolent or foul. Shamans who consciously take the dark work too far in their quest for power or fame, misusing the power of fear to generate results or maliciously harm others, are considered foul. They are a distortion of the light that is all and represent an abuse of shamanic privilege.

While they may have a contractual rapport with their dark allies, giving them access to significant power, they will not have the support of most elementals or guides. Most foul shamans are people who entered into exploring the dark without having properly explored their own shadows first.

What is Shadow?

Heaven and Hell. Angels and Demons. The Light and the Dark. Our spiritual traditions have many stories of the fight between good and evil, cautionary tales that teach us to stay ever in the light. Little Red Riding Hood, Goldilocks. We are taught from early ages that straying into the dark areas of the wood, leaving the well-worn, well-lit paths, will lead us to danger. These stories are well meant, but it is important to explore the darker side of things, too, so that we can truly understand what is light, and what is dark. Often, what we believe to be dark is actually supporting and nourishing us in ways we never imagined. We all have aspects of ourselves that we don't embrace. Behaviors we are less than proud of, habits that we would like to change. We also have parts of ourselves that we love, ways that we act that we think are exemplary, things we do that put us above reproach. Carl Jung explained that our shadow self is "that which we think we are not." We want to believe that we are the light, only the light. But this is not entirely true.

We must begin with the idea that darkness is evil. Source energy is manifested at its highest and truest vibration as light. Lower vibrations of Source energy are "dark", but they are also Source energy. Source energy is everywhere, at all times, in all things. It is never missing. It is never gone. It can't be turned off or excluded from any part or any reality. This is a definitive characteristic of Source energy.

So what defines a vibration as high or low, light or dark? Any being or thing that feels excluded from Source or resists its connection to source energy lowers its vibration. The more connected one feels to Source, the more light one's vibration becomes, and the "lighter" one is. Now, is that person actually more a part of Source than someone else who is trying to turn away from Source energy? No. It's impossible to not be part of Source. You are always part of Source, regardless of what you feel, do or believe. But your thoughts and beliefs create your vibrational status, so the more connected you think you are, the lighter you will feel and become. Conversely, the more disconnected you feel, the darker the shadow you will create as you turn away from Source. This shadow can be cast onto the world around you, lowering the vibration of everything and everyone around you, much like a tree will cast a shadow over a picnic as the sun sets.

Becoming light and raising your vibration is simply a matter of embracing Source energy. All you need to do is invite it into your light with an open heart and mind. The more you resist this light, the more you will feel down and dark. If you are angry, anxious or depressed, that is a good indicator that you are not aligning with Source energy or staying in the moment. Connecting to Source always feels good. Being on your true path and remaining open to the possibilities of creation will always bring joy to yourself and the people around you.

There is a belief in many lightworker circles that everyone you meet is simply a mirror of you, that you create your entire reality and only you are real. This is true in that your reactions to other people can show you what you value in yourself, and what you want to deny or reject. If you hold the belief that lying is always bad, and someone lies to you, you will become very angry and upset. These emotions are a sign that you need to take a moment and get back into the flow of the Universal Source Energy. Most likely you developed this belief when you were punished as a child for lying. You decided right then that you did not want to be "bad", you did not want to be punished, and so you did you best never to lie again. But you were not bad. You cannot be bad. You are Source. So this was a false teaching. You must rise above judgments and a black and white belief system. Source does not judge itself. It embraces all aspects of itself, nurturing the dark into the light, always striving to raise vibration without punitive measures. Some lies are good. Sometimes people are not ready to hear the full truth. The same parents who teach their children to never, ever lie, also lie all the time to those children, sometimes out of convenience, sometimes to create more magic or mystery in their child's life (The Tooth Fairy).

Much of our most positive behaviors arise out of the Dark. We do not like to be hit or made fun of, so we teach our children in that bullying and hitting is bad. We do not like when people will not share with us, and so we are careful to be generous with others. We fear being homeless, so we donate items and money to shelters for people and animals. True compassion derives from empathy, the ability to put oneself in another person's shoes and feel what they feel. This is why it is so important to release a judgmental mindset. You cannot truly feel what another person feels if you are judging them to be below you or evil. Judgment creates darkness as it tries to block out the light. There is light in all beings, in all things. Source is everywhere. No one is truly evil. No one is truly bad. Buddha taught that if you truly loved yourself, you could never hurt another being. A core Buddhist teaching is to be fully enlightened one must first let go of beliefs and judgments based in duality – light/dark, worthy/unworthy, good/bad. To judge someone as bad means that you are also judging Source to be bad, and since you are Source, then you are judging yourself to be bad. This cycle is the birthplace of all negative emotion, all apathy and depression.

You are not bad. You cannot be bad. Let in the light, and allow your emotions to rise.

When we spend time to uncover our darkest aspects, we can bring them into the light. You can see what limiting beliefs you might have that are holding you back, if you have any judgments that regularly lower your vibration and keep you unhappy, and how some of your "dark" aspects actually help make you stronger or better. Once you do this, you embrace your whole self, with your whole heart. Much like when we work with the

Akash, simply identifying patterns and issues can have huge results and instant benefits in our lives. Once something is identified, it can't stayed hidden. Dark pieces are brought into the light through identification, and immediately illuminated by this simple act.

When you allow the light to shine on your darkest pieces, you can begin to see the good in everyone, and release negative patterns of judgment that have been sabotaging your work or your personal life. Relationships will begin to flow more easily. Guilt, shame and anger can be replaced with forgiveness, acceptance and compassion.

Sometimes you will meet people who rub you the wrong way because of something they did in another lifetime, so you cannot always expect to examine their current behavior to decode what is the trigger – this is why working with the

Akash is so important and can give you the deepest healings.

Clearing out Dark Triggers

Dark triggers are judgment based beliefs held deep within the psyche that affect thing you think, feel and do. The best way to identify dark triggers are by finding something that bothers you regularly, say unwashed dishes in the sink when you come home or a fellow employee who is always late to work

Once you have identified your dark trigger, you will see that this deep-held belief can trigger you in a variety situations.

Take a moment to fully *feel* this trigger in your body. Dive deep into the belief. Let it fill you up so you can really feel it, all the anger, sadness, blame, whatever the emotions are that come along with this belief. Feel it and acknowledge the feeling. Tell yourself "I made this feeling. I am the power and the light of the universe, I am all of Source, and I made this feeling. I created this belief. It does not own me. I own it. It has no power over me." Embrace the feeling. It is not wrong or bad. It simply is. Notice the parts of your body where this belief resides, where you feel heavy or uncomfortable. These are areas that might benefit from further energy work after the session is done. Now bring all your light and power into this part of your body, see the light flowing through your crown chakra, flooding through your body and emanating from this space. You are the light.

Akashic and shamanic work can be used to further identify where the belief originated, to help finish the process of clearing it away. To clear the belief out of your system for good, follow up with positive affirmations, EFT (explained below), toning, meditation, reiki or journeywork, just to mention a few options. Remember that adults generally need to practice something 1000 times or more in order to make it a true belief – EFT and affirmations are particularly well-suited for this sort of repetitive work.

The Emotional Freedom Technique

EFT involves tapping on meridian points, which are also chakra and mini chakra points. These centers of energy on the body are where emotions are most likely to be stored. Tapping on the points helps them "wake up" or activate, so that they can more easily release emotions or blockages. When you combine the tapping with affirmations, the tapping helps you to remain more aware of how the body reacts to the words that the mind is forcing it to say. So good body sensations are noticed. Bad sensations are noticed. This gets you in tune with the body as it is meant to be used: as a guide and friend that helps the mind receive guidance from the soul. When the mind is NOT in tune with the soul, or when your words are out of alignment with your desires, then you will feel physical comfort. Pay attention to your body, and seek words and emotions that make you feel great in your body -- then you can flow with life more easily.

EFT is a very good tool for making your body feel appreciated while helping your affirmations penetrate all levels: spirit, mental, physical. EFT brings your body into agreement with your ego and your subconscious while you tap on specific meridian points and you state your affirmations. EFT can involve both positive and negative affirmations, using negative affirmations to reprogram the body towards the positive. The key is for your positive affirmations to be accurate and fully positive. The positive always outweighs the negative. Do not forget to be joy-full while you are tapping!

Below, I outline an EFT example, but I also suggest you check out the internet. There are a lot of great EFT instructional videos on YouTube – I find this the best way to really learn EFT.

How to do an EFT treatment:

While using the four fingers on your dominant hand to tap on the karate chop point, the side of your palm which your pinkie connects to, say the following three times, stating your physical or emotional pain as specifically as possible (this is statement called the "set-up"):

"Even though I _____, I completely love and accept myself." Then tap on each of the following points in order, while saying a positive statement or simply "I love and accept myself"

- Top of the Head/Crown
- Inside of Eyebrow
- Side of eye
- Under eye
- Under nose on the philtrum
- Under your lip above your chin
- Collarbone
- Under the underarm
- Back to top of head.

Here is an example: Perhaps you've been feeling angry when you think about a co-worker named Jim. You could begin with the statement "Even though I am frustrated and angry with Jim, I completely love and accept myself" while you tap on your karate chop point.

Then you'd tap on each of the following points in order with the following statements, beginning with the most accessible or easy to accept statements of feelings first:

- Crown Chakra/Top of the Head, "I love and accept myself."

- Inside of Eyebrow, "I am comfortable at work."

- Side of eye, "I like my co-workers."

- Under eye, "I appreciate it when Jim helps the team."

- Under nose on the philtrum, "I enjoy all my time at work."

- Under your lip above your chin, "It is fun finding new ways to agree and solving problems."

- Collarbone, "I feel at ease and go with the flow at work."

- Under the underarm, "I feel appreciated at work."

- Back to top of head. "I love and accept myself."

EFT works best when repeated often throughout the day. Get creative, and have fun with it.

Freeing the True You

One of the most significant and insidious stumbling blocks to opening our psychic gifts and healing our souls is a lack of self-love. If we cannot fully accept and love ourselves, it is impossible to open our auras fully to world. We are afraid that we will not be accepted. We are afraid that we will not be loved. We're afraid that we will not be valued. We all are capable of empathy, but we do not exercise it all the time. And, we are hardest on ourselves. We are, as many have said before me, our own worst critics. But in order to really tap into mass consciousness and be fully receptive to the information that is out there, we must be willing to open ourselves up and be vulnerable to the possibility that someone else may also tap into us. Many psychic abilities, such as telepathy and mediumship, are a two-way street. We are receiving information, and we are sending information. We are able to tap into Spirit when Spirit is able to tap into us.

There are many ways of helping to strengthen our self-love. The Temple of the Open Heart is a wonderful place to work on various heart-chakra issues. Positive affirmations can work wonders. A dear friend of mine has tapped into her own power by holding a pendulum as she states "I love myself" over and over. The longer she says it, the more vigorously the pendulum swings in a circle – sometimes it even flies out of her hand! She has found that this amplified "love energy" is capable of clearing energy in the rooms throughout her house, and that is helps calm her children down when they are upset.

Another great technique is to give yourself a hug. Cross your arms and place your hands on your shoulders or on your ribcage under your armpits. Holding this position for 20 seconds or longer has been shown to release endorphins and calm the nervous system – not unlike a hug from another person. As you hug yourself, say positive affirmations such as:

I love myself.
I am worthy of love.
I receive love.
I am love.
I am peace.
I release my worries.
I embrace the day.
All is well.

Once mastered, this technique can be used anytime to reaffirm your self-love, even if you hold the position for only a moment. You can also soothe yourself in moments of stress by rubbing your upper arms or sides as you state your affirmations.

Achieving Divine Balance

You have been born into a time of great distortion for the paradigms of masculine and feminine energy, and a time of great healing. It is important, as a healer, to embody these aspects of Source in their most divine forms. The question is, how?

The masculine is the solar, supportive aspect of source. It is the part that nurtures and fuels creation, the energy that drives will. It is best embodied by love and honor.

The feminine is the lunar, creative aspect of source. Ever changing, ever making. It the passionate seed of evolution, the will to expand and manifest.

We know these aspects well in their distortions, where the feminine is receptive and meek, and the male is domineering, angry and controlling. The distortion is the root of much conflict both in personal relationships and the world, and it is our job as shamans to repair it. The male needs to be uplifted by the beauty and passion of the female. When the female does not follow her beauty and passion, then the male becomes uninspired and falls into old, heavy distortions of male patterning. The feminine becomes secondary to the male, when in fact it is the masculine role to support the female as she uplifts the family and the human race at large.

Part of the healing process is to nurture the male and allow its return to its true center of love, protection, and honor. This is no easy task because the distortion of the divine masculine has also distorted the feminine, but it is possible. A simple exercise is to honor the male and female aspects of yourself truthfully and fully with positive affirmations.

Coloring the Aura and Chakras

Sometimes the easiest way to see what is going on with yourself or with another person, is to allow the body itself to show you. Not tell you – but show you. Make a copy of the provided outline, or draw your own, and give the person a full rainbow array of coloring implements (crayons, pastels, markers or colored pencils all work). Ask them to color in the dots on the body, as well as the body itself and around the body. Tell them not to think about it too much, but to simply grab colors without thinking and color away. What you will end up with is an image that will show you what sort of issues are going on and affecting different parts of the body and the chakras, as well as a picture of the aura itself. Use what you have learned about the chakras and the elements and their corresponding colors to intuit what you see. By coloring both the front and back views of the body, you can receive a clearer idea of what is going on.

Remember, there are no "bad" colors, not even black or gray. It is all just information. If you see blue in the root chakra, it does not mean that the chakra is off, but more likely that they are having communication issues about sex or survival – they might need to talk about these issues, or maybe they already are talking about them a lot. Green in the third eye could mean that they use their intuition for healing work, or that they make decisions based on their emotions rather than logic. Black can show grounding or protection. Gray may indicate sadness, but can also be about peace or confusion.

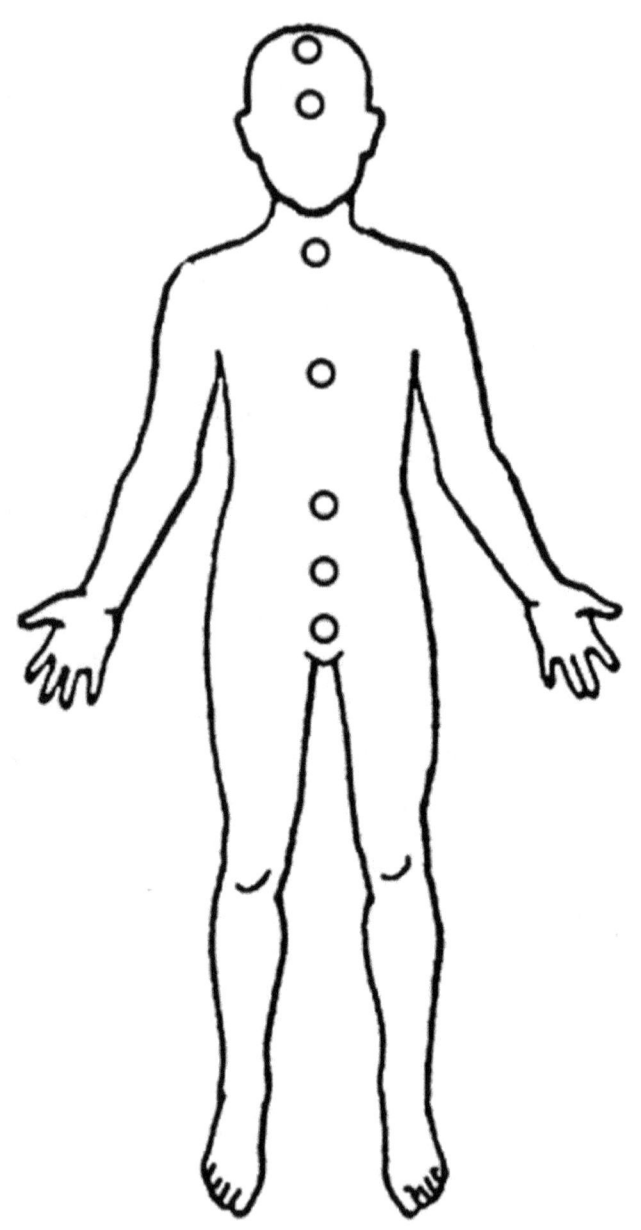

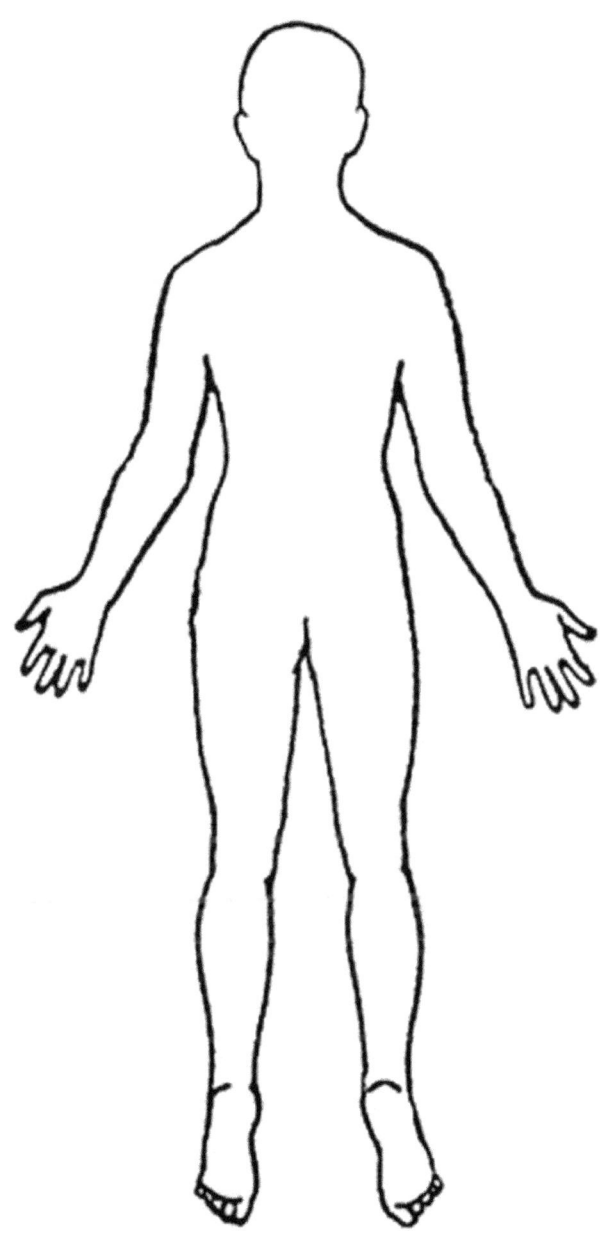

Be the Light

Moving forward, what does a shamanic life look like?

Everyone walks a different path. Where will yours lead?

As a being of immense light and power, remember to stay in the glow of Source. When you feel lost, look to Spirit. When you are rushed and overwhelmed, journey more, not less. When you are distraught and hurting, reach out to your guides – they will do all they can to raise your vibration and shift you towards healing in the easiest manner possible. When you have a choice to make, ask yourself, does this path have a heart? Does it make me feel lighter, or heavier? More, or less, joyful?

Always, follow the joy.

Don't be afraid to take time for yourself, to nurture yourself. The world needs you to be whole. The world needs you to be well. The world needs you to be filled with light and love, shining that blessed radiance that is uniquely YOU all over the place.

Lifting other people up.

Healing the world.

Being you.

About the Author

Maya Cointreau is a certified Reiki master in the Usui tradition, herbalist and a shamanic lightworker with over 20 years of experience. She lives in Connecticut and leads monthly shamanic circles at Enchanted Realms in New Milford (enchantedrealmz.com).

Also by Maya Cointreau:

Simple and Natural Herbal Living
Natural Animal Healing
Equine Herbs and Healing
The Comprehensive Vibrational Healing Guide
The Healing Properties of Flowers
Practical Reiki Symbol Primer
The Girls Who Could Series
Grounding and Clearing
The Mudra Book

More from Earth Lodge:

Lost & Faerie Found
A Child's Collection of Rumi
Number, Name & Color
Shades of Valhalla
Fates of Midgard
Gifts of Aeden
Song Walker
The Warping

www.ingramcontent.com/pod-product-compliance
Lightning Source LLC
LaVergne TN
LVHW051825080426
835512LV00018B/2728